I0463064

Retirement...
The Next Chapter

Helping You Find Financial Direction
for the Next Phase of Life

SCOTT WINSTEAD | COMPASS RETIREMENT

Copyright © 2022 by Scott Winstead.

All rights reserved. No part of this publication may be reproduced, distributed or transmitted in any form or by any means, including photocopying, recording or other electronic or mechanical methods, without the prior written permission of the publisher, except in the case of brief quotations embodied in critical reviews and certain other noncommercial uses permitted by copyright law. For permission requests, write to the publisher at the address below. These materials are provided to you by Scott Winstead for informational purposes only and Scott Winstead and Advisors Excel, LLC expressly disclaim any and all liability arising out of or relating to your use of same. The provision of these materials does not constitute legal or investment advice and does not establish an attorney-client relationship between you and Scott Winstead. No tax advice is contained in these materials. You are solely responsible for ensuring the accuracy and completeness of all materials as well as the compliance, validity, and enforceability of all materials under any applicable law. The advice and strategies found within may not be suitable for every situation. You are expressly advised to consult with a qualified attorney or other professional in making any such determination and to determine your legal or financial needs. No warranty of any kind, implied, expressed or statutory, including but not limited to the warranties of title and non-infringement of third-party rights, is given with respect to this publication.

Scott Winstead/Compass Retirement
www.compassretirement.com
1000 Texan Trail
Suite 213
Grapevine, TX 76051

Book layout ©2020 Advisors Excel, LLC

Retirement . . . The Next Chapter/Scott Winstead. —2nd ed.

ISBN 9781086186680

Scott Winstead is registered as an Investment Advisor Representative and is a licensed insurance agent in numerous states. Compass Retirement is an independent financial services firm that helps individuals create retirement strategies using a variety of investment and insurance products to custom suit their needs and objectives.

Investment advisory services offered only by duly registered individuals through AE Wealth Management, LLC (AEWM). AEWM and Compass Retirement are not affiliated companies.

The contents of this book are provided for informational purposes only and are not intended to serve as the basis for any financial decisions. Any tax, legal or estate planning information is general in nature. It should not be construed as legal or tax advice. Always consult an attorney or tax professional regarding the applicability of this information to your unique situation.

Information presented is believed to be factual and up-to-date, but we do not guarantee its accuracy, and it should not be regarded as a complete analysis of the subjects discussed. All expressions of opinion are those of the author as of the date of publication and are subject to change. Content should not be construed as personalized investment advice nor should it be interpreted as an offer to buy or sell any securities mentioned. A financial advisor should be consulted before implementing any of the strategies presented.

Investing involves risk, including the potential loss of principal. No investment strategy can guarantee a profit or protect against loss in periods of declining values. Any references to protection benefits or guaranteed/lifetime income streams refer only to fixed insurance products, not securities or investment products. Insurance and annuity product guarantees are backed by the financial strength and claims-paying ability of the issuing insurance company.

Any names used in the examples in this book are hypothetical only and do not represent actual clients.

To my mother, my first and best client

To my mother, Theresa Joachim

Table of Contents

The Importance of Planning

Retirement. What is it really? It used to be a time where we quit working at our job after twenty-five to thirty years, stayed home, and waited for the end of life. Today, it has changed. Retirement for most folks today simply means you quit working your 9-to-5 job. You stop going to some mandatory place, sitting in traffic, and having someone to report to. Maybe you plan on starting a second career, or you're ready for the business you've always wanted to pursue. Maybe you plan to travel and spend a lot of time with the grandchildren.

No doubt retirement today looks extremely different than the retirement your parents or grandparents experienced. The extra freedom and choices you have come with the potential for more complexity and worry. Far too often we see people who don't have a plan for their retirement. I believe Lewis Carroll, the great author of *Alice in Wonderland*, said it best regarding a lack of planning:

"If you don't know where you're going, then any road will get you there!"

After over a decade of serving families and helping them plan their retirement, it's been my experience that the majority of people don't have a clear, defined vision of what they actually want their retirement to look like. Sure, it's easy to just say, "I want to travel." But what does that really mean to you? Is that one trip a year? Two trips? Is it domestic or international? Is that getting in an RV and being gone six months of the year? The point is, we have to get very specific about what we want.

The same is true when we think in terms of our income. We usually hear, "I want to keep my lifestyle the same as when I am working." Does that mean trying to replicate the income you make today? Or will you need less income since the house might be paid off at that time? Does it mean you are going to still need as many new clothes as you did when you worked in an office? Will you need the same type of budget for gas and maintenance on your vehicle since you aren't commuting as much?

It is imperative we dive deep into each facet of your retirement and ask as many detailed questions as we can in order to design this next stage of life. For many folks, their retirement plan centers around all the different tools and accounts they have accumulated over the years. Should they have stocks, bonds, annuities, insurance, or real estate? They spend much of their time deciphering and deciding between the tools they could potentially use and not enough time understanding what their goals are.

At Compass Retirement, we spend an extraordinary amount of time helping folks really plan and formulate what their ideal retirement is going to look like. We then help implement the proper strategies that support what they're trying to do and where they're trying to go.

Once we are clear on our vision and understand the correct strategy, it is relatively simple to figure out which tools we need to use. The tools then construct the strategy designed to ultimately achieve your vision!

It is imperative in today's world to have a true retirement plan and not just a bunch of tools that don't all fit together. Remember, if you're not clear on where you want to go, then any road will do ... and it may not be the one you want or desire.

We hope this book will give you valuable insight on many of the most common questions and concerns we hear from retirees today. This insight may help you create and build this next chapter of your life. You've worked way too hard for your possessions and your money. Now is not the time to play guinea pig with your hard-earned dollars and hope it is all just going to magically come together. It might ... and it might not!

Retirement is one of the greatest times in everyone's life. You get to be a kid all over again and do the things you want to do with the people you want to do them with. You also have to have money to create all of those wonderful experiences. When your retirement is properly planned and you know where you want to go, only then will you get to experience the full joy and excitement of this next chapter of your life.

CHAPTER 1

Longevity

You would think the prospect of the grave would loom more frightening as we age, yet many retirees say their number one concern is actually running out of money in their twilight years.[1] This concern is, unfortunately, justified, in part, because of one significant factor: We're living longer.

In 1960, the average life expectancy for a sixty-five-year-old man was seventy-seven, and the average for a sixty-five-year-old woman was eighty. In 2021, men were expected to live to eighty-two and women to eighty-four.[2]

The bottom line of many retirees' budget woes comes down to this: They just didn't plan to live so long. Now, when we are young and in our working years, that's not something we necessarily see as a bad thing; don't some people fantasize about living forever or at least reaching the ripe old age of one hundred?

---

[1] Liz Weston. nerdwallet.com. March 25, 2021. "Will You Really Run Out of Money in Retirement?" https://www.nerdwallet.com/article/finance/will-you-really-run-out-of-money-in-retirement
[2] OECD. 2022. "Life Expectancy at 65." https://data.oecd.org/healthstat/life-expectancy-at-65.htm

However, with a longer lifespan, as we near retirement, we have a few snags. One is that our resources are finite—we only have so much money to provide income—but our lifespans can be unpredictably long, perhaps longer than our resources allow. Also, longer lives don't seem to equate with healthier lives. The longer you live, the more you will need to spend on healthcare, even discounting long-term care needs like nursing homes.

You will also run into inflation. If you don't plan to live another twenty-five years but end up doing so, inflation at an average 3 percent will approximately double the price of goods over that time period. Put a harsh twist on that and the buying power of a ninety-year-old will be half of what they possessed if they retired at sixty-five.[3]

Of course, part of this is that we don't necessarily get to have our cake and eat it, too; our collective increased longevity hasn't necessarily increased the healthy years of our lives. Typically, our life-extending care is most widely applicable to the part of our lives where we will need more care, period. Think of a pacemaker at eighty-five, or radiation pills for cancer at seventy-eight.

"Wow, Scott," I can hear you say, "Way to start with the good news first."

I know, I've painted a fairly grim picture. But all I'm concerned about here is the cost. It's hard to put a dollar sign on life, but that is essentially what we're talking about when we're talking longevity and your

---

[3] Bob Sullivan, Benjamin Curry. Forbes. April 28, 2021. "Inflation And Retirement Investments: What You Need to Know." https://www.forbes.com/advisor/retirement/inflation-retirement-investments

finances. Living longer isn't a bad thing, it just costs more, and one key to a sound retirement strategy is preparing in advance for that expense.

One woman I know illustrates this picture perfectly. Her mother passed away in her late seventies after years of suffering from Alzheimer's disease. Her father died at eighty from cancer. With modern medicine and treatment, this woman survived two rounds of breast cancer, lived with diabetes, and endured a pacemaker, extending her life to age eighty-eight, nearly a decade beyond what she anticipated. However, she and her husband had saved and planned for "just in case," trying to be prepared just in case they had to move, just in case they needed nursing home care, just in case they needed to help children and grandchildren with their expenses. One of their "just-in-case" scenarios was just in case they lived much longer than they anticipated. The last six years of her life were fraught with medical expenses, but she was also blessed with knowing her five great-grandchildren and deepening relationships with her children and grandchildren. She was able to pay for her own medical care, including her final two years in a nursing home, and her twilight years were truly golden. From age eighty-five to eighty-eight, she was more socially active with many visits from family and friends, and she participated in more activities than she had in the seven years since her husband died. When she, too, passed away, her planning from decades earlier allowed her to pass on a legacy to her children, both in ways that can be calculated in dollar signs *and* in ways that can't.

Living longer may be more expensive, but it can be so meaningful when you plan for "what-ifs" and "just-in-cases."

Retiring Later

Planning for a long life in retirement partly comes down to when you retire. While many people end up retiring earlier than they anticipated due to injuries, layoffs, family crises, and other unforeseen circumstances, continuing to work past age sixty and even sixty-five is still a viable option for others and can be an excellent way to help establish financial comfort in retirement.

There are many reasons for this. For one, you obviously still earn a paycheck and the benefits that go with it. Medical coverage and beefing up your retirement accounts with further savings can be pretty significant by themselves, but the advantage of continuing your income is also that it should keep you from dipping into your retirement funds, allowing them the opportunity to grow further.

Additionally, for many workers, their nine-to-five job is more than just clocking in and out. Having a sense of purpose can keep us active physically, mentally, and socially. That kind of activity and level of engagement may also help stave off many of the health problems that plague retirees. Avoiding a sedentary life is one of the advantages of staying plugged into the workforce, if possible.

Our staff met with one man, Rob, three months before he retired. He contacted us, wanting to look at his pension options and put together a plan regarding his income. He had worked for the same employer for over thirty years and was taking their early retirement package at sixty-five. Being married to Mary, who was several years younger, one of his main concerns was making sure she was taken care of in the event he passed away first.

After our initial visit, we formulated a plan for how he was going to have the income he and Mary desired. With the combination of a healthy pension, two Social Security checks, and 401(k) savings, there was no doubt, if managed properly, Rob and Mary would be just fine and not run out of money. Rob submitted the paperwork and set his retirement date. Unfortunately, right after submitting the retirement forms, the stock market dropped considerably. Rob watched his 401(k) savings drop by over $250,000 during that three-month period. This greatly impacted the income plan we had crafted for him and Mary.

After only being "retired" a few months, Rob was back in the job hunt. The only strategy to make their retirement dreams a reality at that point was to go back to work and extend his earning years. Now he is on track to re-retire in the next few years. Sometimes the best remedy for our retirement woes is to work and earn just a little bit longer!

Health Care

Take a second to reflect on your health care plan. Although working up to or even past age sixty-five would allow you to avoid a coverage gap between your working years and Medicare, that may not be an option for you. Even if it is, when you retire, you will need to make some decisions about what kind of insurance coverage you may need to supplement your Medicare. Are there any medical needs you have that may require coverage in addition to Medicare? Did your parents or grandparents have any inherited medical conditions you might consider using a special savings plan to cover?

These are all questions that are important to review with your financial professional so you can be sure you have enough money put aside for health care.

Long-Term Care

Longevity means the need for long-term care is statistically more likely to happen. If you intend to pass on a legacy, planning for long-term care is paramount, since most estimates project nearly 70 percent of Americans turning age 65 today will need some type of it. [4] However, this may be one of the biggest, most stressful pieces of longevity planning I encounter in my work. For one thing, who wants to talk about the point in their lives when they may feel the most limited? Who wants to dwell on what will happen if they no longer can toilet, bathe, dress, or feed themselves?

I get it; this is a less-than-fun part of planning. But a little bit of preparation now can go a long way!

When it comes to your longevity, just like with your goals, one of the important things to do is sit and dream. It may not be the fun, road-trip-to-the-Grand-Canyon kind of dreaming, but spend time envisioning how you want your twilight years to look.

For instance, if it is important for you to live in your home for as long as possible, who will provide for the day-to-day fixes and to-dos of housework if you become ill? Will you set aside money for a service, or

---

[4] LongTermCare.gov. February 18, 2020. "How Much Care Will You Need?" https://acl.gov/ltc/basic-needs/how-much-care-will-you-need

do you have relatives or friends nearby whom you could comfortably allow to help you? Do you have a preference for in-home care over nursing homes or assisted living? This could be a good time to discuss the possibility of moving into a retirement community versus staying where you are, or whether it's worth moving to another state and leaving relatives behind.

These are all important factors to discuss with your spouse and children, as *now* is the right time to address questions and concerns. For instance, is aging in place more important to one spouse than the other? Are the friends or relatives who live nearby emotionally, physically and financially capable of helping you for a time if you have an illness?

Many families I meet with find these conversations very uncomfortable, particularly when children discuss nursing home care with their parents. A knee-jerk reaction for many is to promise they will care for their aging parents. This is noble and well-intentioned, but there needs to be an element of realism here. Does "help" from an adult child mean they stop by and help you with laundry, cooking, home maintenance, and bills? Or does it mean they move you into their spare room when you have hip surgery? Are they prepared to help you toilet and bathe if that becomes difficult for you to do on your own?

I don't mean to discourage families from caring for their own; this can be a profoundly admirable relationship when it works out. However, I've seen families put off planning for late-in-life care based on a tenuous promise that the adult children would care for their parents, only to watch as the support system crumbles. Sometimes this is because the assumed caregiver hasn't given serious thought to the preparation they would need, both in a formal sense and with regard to their personal physical, emotional, and financial commitments. This is often also because we can't see the future: Alzheimer's and other maladies of old age can exact a heavy toll. When a loved one gets to the point he or she is at risk of wandering away or needs help with two or more activities of daily living, it can be more than one person or one family can realistically handle.

If you know what you want, communicate with your family about both the best-case and worst-case scenarios. Then, hope for the best and plan for the worst.

Realistic Cost of Care

Wrapped up in your planning should be a consideration for the cost of long-term care. One study estimates that by 2030, the nation's long-term care costs could reach $2.5 trillion as roughly 24 million Americans require some type of long-term care.[5] The potential costs for such care and treatment can be underestimated, especially by those who have maintained robust health and find it difficult to envision future declines to their condition.

Another piece of planning for long-term care costs is anticipating inflation. It's common knowledge that prices have been and keep rising, which can lower your purchasing power on everything from food to medical

---

[5] Tara O'Neill Hayes, Sara Kurtovic. Americanactionforum.org. February 18, 2020. "The Ballooning Costs of Long-Term Care." https://www.americanactionforum.org/research/the-ballooning-costs-of-long-term-care

care. Long-term care is a big piece of the inflation-disparity pie.

While local costs vary from state to state, here's the national median for various forms of long-term care (plus projections that account for a 3 percent annual inflation, so you can see what I am referencing):[6]

Long-Term Care Costs: Inflation				
	Home Health Care, Homemaker services	Adult Day Care	Assisted Living	Nursing Home (semi-private)
Annual 2021	$59,488	$20,280	$54,000	$94,900
Annual 2031	$79,947	$27,255	$72,571	$127,538
Annual 2041	$107,442	$36,628	$97,530	$171,400
Annual 2051	$144,393	$49,225	$131,072	$230,347

Fund Your Long-Term Care

One big mistake I see are those who haven't planned for long-term care because they assume the government will take care of everything. But that's a big misconception. The government has two health

---

[6] Genworth Financial. January 2022. "Cost of Care Survey 2021." https://www.genworth.com/aging-and-you/finances/cost-of-care.html

insurance programs: Medicare and Medicaid. These can greatly assist you in your healthcare needs in retirement but usually don't provide enough coverage to cover all of your healthcare costs in retirement. My firm isn't a government outpost, so we don't get to make decisions when it comes to forming policy and specifics about either one of these programs. I'm going to give the overview of both, but if you want to get into the details of these programs, you can visit www.Medicare.gov and www.Medicaid.gov.

Medicare

Medicare covers those age sixty-five and older and those who are disabled. Medicare's coverage of any nursing-home-related health issues is limited. It might cover your nursing home stay if it is not a "custodial" stay and it isn't long term. For example, if you break a bone or suffer a stroke and stay in a nursing home for rehabilitative care and then return home, Medicare may cover you. But if you have developed dementia or are looking to move to a nursing facility because you can no longer bathe, dress, toilet, feed yourself, take care of your hygiene, etc., then Medicare is not going to pay for your nursing home costs.[7]

Medicaid

Medicaid is a program the states administer, so funding, protocol, and limitations vary. Compared to Medicare, Medicaid more widely covers nursing home care, but it targets a different demographic than Medicare: those with low incomes.

---

[7] Medicare.gov. "What Part A covers." https://www.medicare.gov/what-medicare-covers/part-a/what-part-a-covers.html.

If you have more assets than the Medicaid limit in your state and need nursing home care, you will need to use those assets to pay for your care. You will also have a list of additional state-approved ways to spend some of these assets over the Medicaid limit, such as pre-purchasing burial plots and funeral expenses, or paying off debts. After that, your remaining assets fund your nursing home stay until they are gone, at which point Medicaid will jump in.

Some people aren't stymied by this, thinking they will just pass on their financial assets early, gifting them to relatives, friends, and causes so they can qualify for Medicaid when they need it. However, to prevent this exact scenario, Uncle Sam has implemented the look-back period. Currently, if you enroll in Medicaid, you are subject to having the government scrutinize the last five years of your finances for large gifts or expenses that may subject you to penalties, temporarily making you ineligible for Medicaid coverage.

So, if you're planning to preserve your money for future generations and retain control of your financial resources during your life, you'll probably want to prepare for the costs of longevity beyond a "government plan."

Self-Funding

One way to fund a longer life is the old-fashioned way, through self-funding. There are a variety of financial tools you can use, and they all have their pros and cons. If your assets are in low-interest but guaranteed vehicles (savings, bonds, CDs), you risk letting inflation erode the value of your dollar. Or, if you are relying on the stock market, you have more growth potential, but you'll also want to consider the possible implications of market volatility; what if your assets take a hit? If you suffer a loss in your retirement portfolio in early or mid-retirement, you might have the option to "tighten your belt," so to speak, and cut back on discretionary spending to allow your portfolio the room to bounce back. But if you are retired and depend on income from a stock account that just hit a downward stride, what are you going to do?

HSAs

These days, you might also be able to self-fund through a health savings account, or HSA, if you have access to one through a high-deductible health plan (you will not qualify to save in an HSA after enrolling in Medicare). In an HSA, any growth of your tax-deductible contributions will be tax-free, and any distributions that are paid out for qualified health costs are also tax-free. That can be a tax trifecta. Long-term care expenses count as health costs, so, if this is an option available to you, that is one way to use the tax advantages to self-fund your longevity. Bear in mind, if you are younger than sixty-five, any money you use for nonqualified expenses will be subject to taxes and penalties, and, if you are older than sixty-five, any HSA money you use for non-medical expenses is subject to income tax.

LTCI

One slightly more nuanced way to pay for longevity, specifically for long-term care, is long-term care insurance, or LTCI. As car insurance protects your assets in case of a car accident, and home insurance protects your assets in case something happens to your house, long-term care insurance aims to protect your assets in case you need long-term care in an at-home or nursing home situation.

As with other types of insurance, you will pay a monthly or annual premium in exchange for an insurance company paying for long-term care down the road. Typically, policies cover two to three years of care, which is adequate for an "average" situation: it's estimated 70 percent of Americans turning age 65 today will need about three years of long-term care of some kind. However, it's important to consider you might not be "average" when you are preparing for long-term care costs; on average, 20 percent of today's sixty-five-year-olds could need care for longer than five years.[8]

Now, there are a few oft-cited components of LTCI that make it unattractive for some:

- Expense — LTCI can be expensive. It is generally less expensive the younger you are, but a fifty-five-year-old couple who purchased LTCI in 2022 could expect to pay $2,080 each year for a benefit of $165,000. And the annual cost only increases from there the older you are.[9]

  Limited options — Let's face it: LTCI may be expensive for consumers, but it can also be

---

[8] LongTermCare.gov. February 18, 2020. "How Much Care Will You Need?" https://acl.gov/ltc/basic-needs/how-much-care-will-you-need

[9] American Association for Long-Term Care Insurance. 2022. "Long-Term Care Insurance Facts-Data-Statistics-2022 Reports" https://www.aaltci.org/long-term-care-insurance/learning-center/ltcfacts-2022.php#2022costs

expensive for companies that offer it. With fewer companies willing to take on that expense, that narrows the market, meaning opportunities to price shop for policies with different options or custom benefits is limited

- If you know you need it, you might not be able to get it — Insurance companies that offer LTCI are taking on a risk that you may need LTCI. That risk is the foundation of the product — you may or may not need it. If you know you will need it because you have a dementia diagnosis or another illness for which you will need long-term care, you will likely not qualify for LTCI coverage.

- Use it or lose it — If you have LTCI and are in the minority of Americans who die having never needed long-term care, all the money you paid into your LTCI policy is gone.

- Possibly fluctuating rates — Your premium rate is not locked in on LTCI. Companies maintain the ability to raise or lower your premium amounts. This means some seniors face an ultimatum: Keep funding a policy at what might be a less affordable rate OR lose coverage and let go of all the money they paid in thus far.

After that, you might be thinking, "How can people possibly be interested in LTCI?" But let me repeat myself—as many as 70 percent of Americans age 65 today will need long-term care. And, although only one in ten Americans age 55 and over have purchased LTCI, keep in mind the high cost of nursing home care. Can you afford $7,000 a month to put into nursing home care and still have enough left over to protect your legacy? This is a very real concern considering one set of statistics reported a two-in-three chance that a senior citizen will become physically or cognitively impaired in their lifetime.[10] So, not to sound like a broken record, but it is vitally important to have a plan in place to deal with longevity and long-term care if you intend to leave a financial legacy.

While LTCI can help solve certain needs, there are often better ways to pay for care. Even those who understand the need to plan for LTC don't want to pay for something they might not use. Here enters Life Insurance with Accelerated Death Benefit (ADB). If someone is diagnosed as terminally ill, the ADB rider can be payable in advance of their death for any purpose, including home care, assisted living, and hospice. ADB beneficiaries still receive a death benefit, although it is reduced by the amount of the ADB. And if the rider is never exercised, then the life insurance company pays the beneficiaries a tax-free death benefit.[11]

There is another LTCI alternative: the long-term care rider. You can add this rider onto your life insurance policy as well. Here's how it works. Let's pretend we have a $100,000 life insurance policy with a long-term care rider. If we qualify for care, we can access the $100,000 early to cover costs associated with things such as in-home care, assisted living, adult day care, and, of course, nursing home care. Now, let's

---

[10] payingforseniorcare.com. 2022. "Long-Term Senior Care Statistics" https://www.payingforseniorcare.com/statistics
[11] Christina Drumm Boyd. Paying For Senior Care. September 22, 2020. "Life Insurance Accelerated Death Benefits: Pros & Cons." https://www.payingforseniorcare.com/financial-products/insurance

pretend we used $50,000 of our life insurance proceeds while we were alive for our care. We then pass away. The remaining $50,000 passes on to our family or beneficiaries as tax-free inheritance! It might be the only thing you ever purchase where you know someone is going to receive a benefit. Either you are going to use it while you are alive for your care or someone will receive the money when you pass away. Make no mistake, someone is going to benefit!

Understandably, a discussion on long-term care and its particulars is bound to feel at least a little tedious. Yet, this is a crucial piece of planning for income in retirement, particularly if you want to leave a legacy.

Four years ago, we met Ted at a large church event we were asked to speak at. The topic of discussion that afternoon was titled "The Long-Term Care Crisis Coming for You." After we gave the presentation, Ted approached and emphatically demanded he come see us to receive more information similar to what he had just heard.

Ted scheduled his appointment for the following Tuesday. I entered the conference room with my cup of coffee, eager to meet Ted. Before I could even sit down and exchange pleasantries, Ted said, "I just want you to know I am only here to understand the long-term care stuff. I am not sharing any of my personal financial information with you. I have an advisor I have known for over twenty-five years. We golf together, eat lunch together, and I am not making any changes!"

"Ted, buddy," I said, "can I take a seat first?"

We sat down. I asked him, "What do you want to know about long-term care that we didn't cover last week at the seminar?"

"Well," he replied, "my advisor said I can't get long-term care insurance, and I need it."

We had been doing this long enough to know most people don't have a sense of urgency around getting LTCI. I decided to inquire further.

"Why do you think you need long-term care insurance so badly?"

"My wife, Lisa, is sixteen years younger than me, and I think I will die before she does, so I want to make sure she is taken care of."

"I am curious, Ted, why did your current advisor tell you that you couldn't get long-term care insurance?"

"Well," Ted said, "I just was diagnosed with early-onset Parkinson's disease."

His current broker was correct. Ted didn't qualify for long-term care insurance with Parkinson's disease.

"Would it be helpful if I showed you another way we could look at getting coverage for your care?"

"That's why I am here," he said.

I explained to Ted that there were certain types of life insurance where he could purchase an additional long-term care rider and then use some of the policy's value early for his care if he needed to. *If* he never needed care, then the life insurance would pay his wife and/or family any remaining death benefit when he passed away.

"I have never heard of this before," Ted stated.

"Well, that's the difference between working with a true retirement planner versus an investment broker," I said. "A retirement planner knows not only about your investments, but also your healthcare, long term care, taxes, estate planning, etc. It is way more than just managing your portfolio."

Ted was someone who needed strategies outside of what his current financial professional was offering. After talking to him that first time, it was easy for me to think of alternatives to traditional long-term care insurance that might fit his needs.

Find a professional who understands your needs and goals and also understands there are many different ways to solve this problem. If you don't know any, call us. However you choose to plan, just make sure you have one. This is an issue coming for all of us in some form or fashion!

Spousal Planning

One thing to keep in mind no matter how you plan to save: Many of us will be planning for more than ourselves. Look back at all the stats on health events and the likelihood of long life and long-term care. If they hold true for a single individual, then the likelihood of having a costly health or long-term care event is even higher for a married couple. And you'll be planning for not just one life but two. So, when it comes to long-term care insurance, life insurance with an ADB, a long-term care rider, self-funding, or whatever strategy you are looking at utilizing, be sure you are funding longevity for both of you.

So often we want to make sure there is a plan in place for both spouses. However, when planning for long-term care, we really want to emphasize how important it is for the wife. Typically in a marriage, who gets sick first? That's right, it's usually the husband. And, like a nurturing, caring, and loving wife, she will spend every penny making sure he is taken care of until the end of his life. Then he passes away, and she has spent all the money on his care. What is she left with? Probably a lot less than before, and, often, she could even qualify as destitute. To avoid this scenario, we have to make sure we insure her longevity and care.

Not too many years ago, we had the pleasure of serving Patty and Bill. We hit it off immediately. Not only were they serious about putting a plan in place for retirement, they were also just an amazing couple. They knew they needed a plan for their care. Patty told us what they wanted, and it was something we hear from clients nearly every day. When asking about the goal someone has for care, the number one response we hear is, "We just don't want to be a burden to our children!"

To that end, Bill and Patty walked through the process to see if they would qualify for life insurance with the ADB. Patty qualified with flying colors; unfortunately, Bill did not qualify at all. He was greatly disappointed.

This happens from time to time, and our office has learned to be prepared to alter plans and move ahead with a Plan B, when needed. One option in a case such as this would be to self-fund. In the case of self-funding, our office would be sure the income plan was in place, and then we'd come up with a realistic estimate of how much care the uninsured party might need and set aside money for that care. That way, the insured person would feel free to spend money on their spouse's care and rest easy knowing they, too, are covered. Remember, the time to plan for these costs is now—not later!

Our stance at Compass Retirement is simple. You will never be as young and healthy as you are today. Do not put this planning off! Take action and rest easy.

CHAPTER 2

Taxes

W here to begin with taxes? Perhaps by acknowledging we all bear responsibility for the resources we share. Roads, bridges, schools . . . It is the patriotic duty of every American to pay their fair share of taxes. Many would agree with me, though, while they don't mind paying their fair share, they're not interested in paying one cent more!

Now, just talking taxes probably takes your mind to April, tax season. You are probably thinking about all the forms you collect and how you file. Perhaps you are thinking about your certified public accountant or another qualified tax professional and saying to yourself, "I've already got taxes taken care of, thanks!"

However, what I see when people come into my office is that their relationship with their tax professional is purely a January through April relationship. That means they may have a tax professional, but not a tax *planner*.

What I mean by that is tax planning extends beyond filing taxes. In April, we are required to do an accounting with the IRS to make sure we have paid up on our bill or to settle the score if we have overpaid. But real tax planning is about making each financial move in a way that allows you to keep the most money in your pocket and out of Uncle Sam's.

Now, as a caveat, I want to emphasize that I am not a CPA, nor am I a tax planner, but I see the way taxes affect my clients, and I have plenty of experience helping clients with tax-efficient strategies in their retirement plans, in conjunction with their tax professionals.

It is especially important to me to help my clients develop tax-efficient strategies in their retirement plans because each dollar they can keep in their pockets is a dollar we can put to work.

"There are only two certainties in life, death and taxes!" Do you know who originally said that? If you said Benjamin Franklin, you are correct. As a retirement planner, we absolutely *hate* that quote. Nothing against Ben Franklin, but that saying makes us feel powerless. Unfortunately, none of us have any idea how or control over when we die. When you lump anything with a comparison to death, it makes it feel as if we have lost all control.

That isn't true for taxes. While it is true we don't set the tax brackets or tax rates (Congress does that), we have one hundred percent control over our income. By controlling how your income is distributed, you can, in many ways, control your taxation. As mentioned earlier, there are only three things you really have control over in your retirement: The fees you pay, the risk you take, and the taxes you owe. The higher those three variables are, the less money you have. The lower they are, the more money you have, regardless of whether the stock market goes up, down, or sideways. Understanding your income and the tax code puts all the power back into our hands . . . not the hands of the IRS.

Let us ask you a question, "What do you think taxes are going to do over the course of your lifetime? Go up? Go down? Stay the same?" While it is impossible to know for sure, we believe taxes will continue to rise over our lifetime.

What's Our Debt?

Now, in the United States, taxes can be a rather uncertain proposition. Currently, it would be easy to assume tax rates will decline in the next four to eight years. However, there is one (large!) factor that we, as a nation, must confront: the national debt.

According to USDebtClock.org, we are over $30,000,000,000,000 in debt and climbing. That's $30 TRILLION with a T. With just $1 trillion, you could park it in the bank at a zero percent interest rate and still spend more than $54 million every day for fifty years without hitting a zero balance. Now take that times twenty-two.

Even if Congress got a handle and stopped that debt from its daily compound, divided by each taxpayer, we each would owe about $244,000. So, will that be check or cash?

Remembering back to my college economics class, when we have debt, there are two options we can choose to fix it. First, we can print more money. When we do that, it causes inflation. Hopefully you know as well as I do that, when you are on a fixed income in retirement, inflation can silently strangle you. Second, the U.S. can raise taxes. That's it; those are the options.

There isn't really any other option to start to claw our way out as a country.

My point here isn't to give you anxiety. I'm just saying, even with the rosiest of outlooks on our personal income tax rates, you cannot count on low tax rates for the long term. Instead, you and your network of professionals (tax, legal, and financial) should constantly be looking for ways to take advantage of tax-saving opportunities as they come. After all, the best "luck" is when proper planning meets opportunity.

So, how can we get started?

Know Your Limits

One of the foundational pieces of tax planning is knowing what tax bracket you are in based on your income after subtracting pre-tax or untaxed assets. Your income taxes are based on your taxable income.

One reason to know your income tax rate is so you can see how far away you are from the next lower or higher tax bracket. This is particularly important when it comes to decisions such as gifting and Roth IRA rollovers. You will want to be sure to talk to a tax professional and a financial advisor registered to provide investment advice before making any decisions.

For instance, based on the 2022 tax table, Mallory and Ralph's taxable income was just over $345,000, putting them in the 32 percent tax bracket and $4,900 above the upper end of the 24 percent tax bracket. They already maxed out their retirement funds' tax-exempt contributions for the year. Their daughter, Gloria, is a sophomore in college. They could shave a considerable amount off their tax bill by using that $4,900 to help

Gloria out with groceries and school—something they were likely to do anyway, but now can deliberately put to work for them in their overall financial strategy as a tax-exempt gift.

Now, I use Mallory and Ralph only as an example—your circumstances may be different—but I think this nicely illustrates the way planning ahead for taxes can save you money.

Assuming a Lower Tax Rate? Big Mistake

Many people anticipate being in a lower tax bracket in retirement. It makes sense: You won't be contributing to retirement funds, you'll be drawing from them. And you won't have all those work expenses—work clothes, transportation, etc.

Yet, do you really plan on changing your lifestyle after retirement? Do you plan to cut down on the number of times you eat out, scale back vacations, and skimp on travel?

What I see in my office is that many couples spend more in the first few years, or maybe the first decade, of retirement. Sure, later on, that may taper off, but usually only just in time for their budget to be reduced by health and long-term care expenses. Do you see where this is going? Many people plan as though their taxable income will be lower in retirement and are surprised when the tax bills come in and look more or less the same as they used to. It's better to plan for the worst and hope for the best, wouldn't you agree?

Tax-Free vs Taxable

I played soccer in college. In my senior year, as I was preparing to graduate, all I thought about was playing professionally. That season, I broke my leg, and my soccer career tragically ended. Not knowing what I was going to do after graduation, I began putting together my resumé. After applying for jobs, I was hired by a large healthcare company and started immediately upon graduation. My position required a ton of travel each week, and my pay was pretty low. But, I was grateful to have this job. I was twenty-two, recently graduated, and didn't have any money to my name.

Walking into the office for the first time, Linda, the human resources specialist, greeted me and took me to the conference room. There, she gave me a welcome packet and walked me around the building. When we returned to the conference room, I signed my employment contract, and Linda asked if I wanted to sign up for their retirement plan.

"Scott, do you want to start saving for your retirement?" she asked.

"Um, OK," I said. "How do I do that?"

"We have a 401(k) plan here, and we deduct some money from your paycheck each pay period. You don't have to pay any taxes on the money, and we put it in an account for you. You get to pick all the investments and eventually, when you retire, you will have a lot of funds to use."

Now, I was twenty-two and broke, so this sounded pretty good. I was always taught to make sure I understood things before I signed any documents, so I replied, "Sure, Linda, that sounds good. I heard you say that I don't pay any taxes on the money, so, just to clarify, when does the company pay those taxes for me?"

I am sure you just laughed a little bit due to my naivety . . . It's okay, so did Linda.

"Scott, the company doesn't pay the taxes. You will pay them, but only when you take money out of the account."

I thought about this for a minute and told Linda I would politely decline the offer to participate in the 401(k) plan. Very surprised, she asked why.

"Well, I don't think I want an account with a lot of money in it that I have to pay a bunch of taxes on in thirty-five years. It just doesn't sound like a good deal," I said.

The next words that came out of Linda's mouth are something I am sure you have heard someone say over the course of your working life. She very emphatically stated...

"Scott, don't worry about paying the taxes later because, when you take the money out, you will be in a lower tax bracket than you are today!"

Have you ever heard someone tell you that? Put your money in these tax-deferred accounts, and then, when you withdraw the money, you will be in a lower tax bracket. After being a retirement planner for over a decade, I feel strongly this is not true for most people. I was twenty-two at the time and was going to be making very little income. I was never going to be in a lower tax bracket than I was at that time in my life. Is that true for you, too? Are you in a lower tax bracket today than when you started shoving money into your 401(k), traditional IRA, 403(b), or any of these other pre-taxed accounts in your twenties, thirties, forties, or even fifties? My guess is probably not.

In my opinion, these tax-deferred accounts are very tax-*inefficient* to own in retirement and distribute money out of. Why? Because they are rule-based accounts. And, who do you think makes the rules? Us or the federal government? That's right, the federal government.

The rule that makes 401(k) and traditional IRA accounts sound attractive is that they are tax-deferred. Make no mistake, they are not tax-*free*. Very rarely is anything free of taxation, when you get down to it. Using 401(k)s and IRAs in retirement is no different. The taxes the government deferred when you were in your working years are now coming due, and you will pay taxes on that income at whatever your current tax rate is.

Just to ensure Uncle Sam gets his due, the government also has a required minimum distribution, or RMD, rule. Beginning at age seventy-two, you are required to withdraw a certain minimum amount every year from your 401(k) or IRA, or else you will face a 50 percent tax penalty on any RMD monies you should have withdrawn but didn't, and that's on top of income tax. Each year from the time you turn age seventy-two, the amount you have to take from these accounts increases.

If you believe taxes will rise over the course of your life, then you will likely report more and more income at a potentially higher tax rate the older you get. Does that sound like a good thing for you, or for the IRS? Also, let us not forget that the more income you show on your tax return, the more your Social Security income is taxed and your Medicare premiums may be higher . These RMDs can cause stress, especially if you don't even need the money for income. In our experience, a lot of folks don't even need these distributions. If it were up to them, they would just leave them in the account, but they can't. Take a guess what most people do with these withdrawals if they don't need the money to live on. Do you think they spend it? Do you think they put it in the bank? What do most people do? In my experience, they tend to invest it.

Here's the deal . . . if you weren't a big spender while you were working, you don't typically start spending big in retirement. You probably aren't going to put it in the bank, either, because you don't earn much return in that kind of account. So, you might just invest it, hoping to gain a return on your money.

So, let's think about this strategically. Let's say I have a retirement account the government forces me to take a withdrawal from. When the money comes out, I have to report it as income and pay income tax on it. I then give whatever amount is remaining to my broker or financial advisor to invest for me so when that investment grows and I sell it or collect a dividend I can pay . . . that's right, *more taxes*!

We see this every day, and it's so unnecessary. We have to get out of the cycle of paying taxes on the same dollar two and even three separate times!

That's where the power of tax-free accounts come in. You need as many tax-free shelters for your money as possible and as appropriate to your situation. You need a place where your money can grow tax-free, you can withdraw it tax-free, and you can pass it on tax-free. There are only three places where that exists today.

1. Roth IRA/Roth 401(k)
2. Municipal Bonds[12]
3. Permanent Life Insurance[13]

That's it.

We will cover all of these more in-depth later, but let's briefly take a look at the Roth IRA since we've been discussing other IRAs. You can think of the difference between a Roth and a traditional IRA as the difference between taxing the seed and taxing the harvest. Because Roth IRAs are funded with dollars that have already been taxed, there aren't tax penalties for early withdrawals of the principal, nor are there taxes on the growth after you reach age fifty-nine-and-one-half. And, perhaps best of all, there are no RMDs. Of course, you must own a Roth account for a minimum of five years before you are able to take advantage of all of its features.

This is one more area where it pays to be aware of your tax bracket. Some people may find it advantageous to "convert" their traditional retirement account funds to a Roth IRA in a year they are in a lower tax bracket. Others may opt to put any excess RMDs from their traditional retirement accounts into other products, like stocks or insurance.

Does that make your head spin? Understandable. That's why it's so important to work with a financial professional and tax planner who can help you not only

---

[12] Municipal bonds may not be exempt from both state and federal taxes. Consult with your tax advisor for details.

[13] Permanent life insurance allows its cash value to grow on a tax-free basis. Death benefits are paid to your beneficiary tax-free. Any available cash values can be withdrawn tax-free as a loan or policy withdrawal, assuming the policy is not a Modified Endowment contract. Policy loans and withdrawals will reduce the policy death benefit and cash values and may cause the policy to lapse.

execute these sorts of tax-efficient strategies but also help you understand what you are doing and why.

Market Volatility

U p and down. Roller coaster. Merry-go-round. Bulls and bears. Peak-to-trough.

Sound familiar? This is the language we use to talk about the stock market. With volatility and spikes, even our language is jarring, bracing, vivid.

Still, financial strategies tend to revolve around market-based products, for good reasons. For one thing, there is no other financial class that packs the same potential for growth, pound for pound, as stock-based products. Growth potential, outpacing inflation, new opportunities . . . for these reasons, it may be unwise to avoid the market entirely.

However, along with the potential for growth is the potential for loss. Many of the people I see in my office come in still feeling a bit burned from the market drama of 2000 to 2010. The market shot back up in the years that followed, but the bumps of 2018 brought us back down to earth a little. If that didn't prove the markets are impossible to predict, the first quarter of 2020 certainly did, when COVID-19 changed the financial outlook of many investors.

So how do we balance these factors? How do we try to satisfy both the need for protection and the need for growth?

For one thing, it is important to recognize the value of diversity. Now, I'm not just talking about the diversity of assets among different kinds of stocks, or even different kinds of stocks and bonds. That's only one kind of diversity; while important, both stocks and bonds, though different, are still market-based products. Just as an incoming tide raises all boats, most market-based products tend to rise or lower as a whole. Thus, diversity among stocks and bonds won't automatically protect your assets during times when the market as a whole declines.

In addition to the sort of "horizontal diversity" you have by purchasing a variety of stocks and bonds from different companies, I encourage having "vertical diversity," or diversity among asset classes. This means having different product types, including both securities products and insurance products, with varying levels of growth potential, liquidity, and protection—all in accordance with your unique situation, goals, and needs.

Remember, risk is one of the three things we can control within our retirement. The other two are taxes and fees.

We like to think of risk this way. Imagine driving down a stretch of highway. It's a beautiful day, the sun is shining, and your favorite song is playing. Imagine you are only going twenty miles per hour, like in a school zone. At this speed you really aren't in jeopardy of losing control of the car, but, even if you did, there are guardrails on the side of the road to keep you safe and in line—almost like bumpers on the lane in a bowling alley. If you were to get in an accident under this scenario, the results would probably be a minor fender bender or irritation, but nothing serious.

Now, suppose you are traveling down the same stretch of highway, sun shining, music playing. Only this time you are driving eighty miles per hour. You are whizzing by all the other cars as if they are standing still. Things are moving really fast, and there isn't really any room for error. The guardrails are non-existent. You could careen off the road and end up in a ditch any moment. If you were to get in an accident at this point, things could be catastrophic and tragic!

This is exactly how you need to think about risk within your retirement. One of the things we help people do is figure out what their appropriate speed is and, more importantly, what their speed *limit* is. Too slow and you aren't making enough money to keep up. Too fast and you could get seriously hurt when the market drops. Secondly, we help them determine how far away they want their "guardrails" built from their retirement lane. The closer they are, the fewer the swings and calmer the ride. The further away they are, the more upside they might have—as well as more downside. In our experience, many people are traveling at a far faster speed than they intend. And, they almost certainly wish they had their guardrails much closer than they actually are.

When assessing risk, it is imperative to ask yourself, "How much am I willing to lose over a given time period?" The answer is different for everyone and can even be different per account. The success of your retirement is not about the money you make, it's about the money you *keep*!

Your Retirement Buckets

When you're looking at your overall portfolio diversity, part of the equation is knowing which products fit in what category: where is the protection, what will generate my income, and what has growth potential.

Before we dive in, keep in mind these aren't absolutes. You might think of protection, market, and income as colors. While some products will look pretty much green, red, or blue, others will have a mix of characteristics, making them more turquoise or purple.

Protection Bucket

Green is my protected, or guaranteed, category color. I typically recommend having at least enough green money to cover six months' to a year's worth of expenses in case of emergency. Green assets don't need a lot of growth potential; they just need to be readily available when we need them.

- Cash
- Money market accounts

Income Bucket

The color of income, to me, is blue. Tranquil, peaceful, sure, even if it lacks a certain amount of flash. This is the direction I like to see people move toward as they're nearing retirement. The red, flashy look of stock market returns, and the risk of possible overnight losses is less attractive as we near retirement and look for more consistency and reliability. While this category doesn't come with a lot of liquidity, the products here are backed by an insurance company, a bank or a government entity.

- Certificates of deposit (bank)
- Government-based bonds (government)
- Life insurance (insurance company)
- Annuities (insurance company)

Market Bucket

I like to think of the market category as red. It's powerful, it's somewhat volatile, and it's also the category where we have the biggest opportunity for growth and loss. Sometimes products in the market category have a good deal of liquidity but very little protection. These are our market-based products and strategies, so we're thinking mostly shades of red and orange. This is a good place to be when you're young — think fast cars and flashy leather jackets — but its allure often wanes as you get move closer to retirement.

- Stocks
- Equities
- Exchange-traded funds
- Mutual funds
- Corporate bonds
- Real estate investment trusts
- Speculations
- Alternative investments

Our philosophy is that you most people should have money in all three buckets. It is important to make sure you have your Protection (green) and Income (blue) buckets taken care of first. When you know you have plenty in an emergency fund, available for you to grab at a moment's notice, then you can relax. The same is true in knowing some of your money is protected and is going to generate the income you need to live on. This income needs to stay steady, keep up with inflation, and support both spouses. The goal of this income bucket is to provide for you above and beyond what Social Security or your pension provides.

Once these two things are set up, everything else can go into the Market (red) bucket. This bucket gives us the best chance for growth over time, though it is never a straight line upward. It might make money one year and lose more the next. Since we don't know when those years will be, we have to put ourselves in a position to not need to touch the red bucket money in a "down" year. This can be a problem if you have some of those tax-deferred accounts (i.e., 401(k), traditional IRA, 403(b), etc.) in the red bucket. When those mandatory distributions start, we have to take money out whether we want to or not. It is at this moment when mistakes—and market downfalls—can become magnified.

Suppose you have to withdraw 4 percent out of your 401(k) or traditional IRA? Let's assume the market earned 10 percent that year. You withdrew 4 percent and the market made 10 percent. How much did your account actually make? If you said 6 percent, you are correct. Now, assume you withdrew the same 4 percent, only this time the market dropped by 10 percent. You took 4 percent and the market took 10 percent. How much did your account go down by? That's right . . . 14 percent. This is one way people run out of money in retirement. When you withdraw money from an account, the good years and the bad years become *realized*. We lock in either the gain or the loss, but, either way, it is no longer *unrealized*. Think back to 2008. The S&P 500 fell 38 percent that year. If you withdrew 4 percent that year, then you incurred a 42 percent loss . . . *in one year*! If you pay a fee of 1 to 2 percent, add that in as well. At that point, *hope* becomes your new strategy.

Control your risk, and you control your retirement. Neglect your risk, and your retirement is left up to chance!

CHAPTER 4

Retirement Income

R etirement. For many of us, it's what we've saved for and dreamed of, pinning our hopes to a magical someday. Is that someday full of traveling? Is it filled with grandkids? Gardening? Maybe your fondest dream is just never having to work again, never having to clock in or be accountable to someone else.

Your ability to do these things all hinges on *income*. Why? Because income gives us *choice*. The more income you have in retirement, the better trips you take, the better care you receive, and the more time you get to spend with your family. Income equals choice, and we all love having choices. No one wants to be told they can't do or have something. Without the money to support these dreams, even a basic level of work-free lifestyle is unsustainable. That's why planning for your income in retirement is so foundational. But where to begin?

It can be easy to feel overwhelmed by this question. Some may feel the urge to amass a large lump sum and then try to put it all in one product—insurance, investments, liquid assets—to provide all the growth, liquidity, and income they need. Instead, we think you need a more balanced approach. After all, retirement planning isn't magic. There is no single product that can be all things to all people, or even all things to one person, and no approach works unilaterally for everyone. That's why it's important to talk to a financial professional who can help you lay down the basics and take you step-by-step through the planning process. Not only will you have the assurance that you have addressed the areas you need to, but you will also have an ally who can help you break down the process and help keep you from feeling overwhelmed.

Sources of Income

Thinking of all the pieces of your retirement expenses might be intimidating. But, like cleaning out a junk drawer or revisiting that garage remodel, once you have laid everything out, you can begin to sort things into categories.

Once you have a good overall picture of where your expenses will lie, you can start stacking up the resources to cover them.

Social Security

Social Security is a guaranteed, inflation-protected federal insurance program playing a significant part in most of our retirement plans. From delaying until you've reached full retirement age or beyond to examining spousal benefits, as I discuss elsewhere in this book, there is plenty you can do to try to make the most of this monthly benefit. As with all your retirement income sources, it's important to consider how to make this resource stretch to provide the most bang and buck for your situation.

Pension

Another generally reliable source of retirement income for you might be a pension, if you are one of the lucky people who still have them.

If you don't have a pension, go ahead and skim on down to the next point; but if you do have a pension, let's take a second to expand on your options.

Because your pension can be such a central piece of your retirement income plan, you will want to put some thought into answering basic questions about it.

How well is your pension funded? Since the heyday of the pension plan, many companies and governments have neglected to fund their pension obligations, causing a persistent problem with this otherwise reliable asset. However, research conducted by the Pew Charitable Trusts showed a collective increase in assets exceeding half a trillion dollars in state retirement plans fueled by strong market investment returns in fiscal 2021. Pew's estimates that state retirement systems rose to 80 percent funding for the first time in 2008.[14]

Consider the factors at play, though. Pensions had been underfunded and gained a boost from strong market performance in 2021. What happens to the solvency of those pension funds if the market declines?

It can be worthwhile to keep tabs on your pension's health and know what your options are for withdrawing your pension. If you have already retired

---

[14] pewtrusts.org. September 14, 2021. "The State Pension Funding Gap: Plans Have Stabilized in Wake of Pandemic" https://www.pewtrusts.org/en/research-and-analysis/issue-briefs/2021/09/the-state-pension-funding-gap-plans-have-stabilized-in-wake-of-pandemic

and made those decisions, this may be a foregone conclusion. If not, it pays to know what you can expect and what decisions you can make, such as taking spousal options to cover your husband or wife if he or she outlives you.

Also, some companies are incentivizing lump-sum payouts of pensions to reduce the companies' payment liabilities. If that's the case with your employer, talk to your financial professional to see if that option is viable for you or if it might be better to stick with lifetime payments or other options.

Your 401(k) and IRA

One "modern way" to save for retirement is in a 401(k) or IRA (or their nonprofit or governmental equivalents). These tax-advantaged accounts are, in my opinion, a poor substitute for pensions, but one of the biggest disservices we do to ourselves is to not take full advantage of them in the first place. According to one article, only 41 percent of Americans invest in a 401(k), though 68 percent of employed Americans have access to a 401(k) benefit option.[15]

Also, if you have changed jobs over the years, do the work of tracking down any benefits from your past employers. You might have an IRA here or a 401(k) there; keep track of those so you can pull them together and look at those assets when you're ready to look at establishing sources of retirement income.

---

[15] Amin Dabit. personalcapital.com. April 1, 2021. "The Average 401k Balance by Age."
https://www.personalcapital.com/blog/retirement-planning/average-401k-balance-age

Other Assets

- Do you have life insurance?
- Do you have any annuities?
- How about long-term care insurance?
- Any passive income sources?
- Stock and bond portfolios?
- Liquid assets? What's in your bank account?
- Any alternative investments?
- How about rental properties?

It's important, if you are going through the work of sitting with a financial professional, to look at your entire retirement income picture—to pull together ALL of your assets, no matter how big or small. From the free insurance policy offered at your bank to the sizeable investment in your brother-in-law's modestly successful furniture store, you want to have a good idea of where your money is.

Chris came to see us a few years ago. He was in the telecommunications industry and made a comfortable living. He and his wife, April, lived within their means and were responsible savers. They had two grown children and a granddaughter.

One of Chris and April's main concerns was figuring out how to structure their income in retirement. They just couldn't piece together how the income they wanted was going to be achieved. Before we started, the first thing we had to establish was a very special number every single one of us possesses. That number is: the sit-on-the-porch number.

What is Your Sit-on-the-Porch Number?

You may never have heard of the sit-on-the-porch number. If you haven't, let us explain. For every single one of us, there is some amount of money it takes for us to just comfortably sit on our porch each month. We are not talking about vacations, eating out, giving gifts, etc. We are talking about the amount of money it takes you each month for your basic necessities. Utilities, food, shelter, insurance, taxes, etc. That number is different for each of us. Yours might be $5,000 per month. It could be $3,000 per month. There is no right or wrong here. It is how much it will cost you just to function each month. Before we can plan our income, we have to know what that number is. It serves as the foundation of our income plan. It is crucial for you to have a steady, guaranteed way of knowing this amount of money will be there for you over the course of your lifetime . . . no matter how long you live. It also has to inflate (more on this later), and it has to sustain both spouses.

Think back to our Social Security discussion. If you and your spouse both have Social Security and one of you passes away first, what happens to one of the Social Security payments? That's right, it goes away. That is not the time you want to take a hit to your income when you or your loved ones are grieving. Your income plan has to take this into account.

Goals and Dreams: Does the Tail Wag the Dog?

Does the tail wag the dog or the dog wag the tail? Well, over 80 percent of people we help allow the tail to wag the dog. They focus on products, investments, assets . . . we call them the *tools*. Yes, tools are important, but they are only something to be used to achieve your *goals* and *dreams*! If you aren't clear on what you are trying to accomplish or where you want to go, how do you know if you are using the appropriate tool? Too often we receive questions like:

"Should I use a mutual fund?"

"Is this annuity any good?"

"Should I get long-term care insurance?"

These are all good questions; however, the answer is *maybe* for every single one of them. Those are all just tools. They are neither good nor bad. What makes them either effective or ineffective is how they are applied to your *goals*! Listen, if we laid a hammer on the table and I picked it up and hit myself in the head, I would say hammers are horrible and you shouldn't ever use a hammer. But if I picked up that same hammer and used it to drive a nail into the wall to hang a beautiful picture, I would say, "This is the greatest tool ever! Look how efficient and easy it made my job."

The point is, the hammer didn't change at all. The only thing that changed was how I applied it to my goals!

I like to start with your pie in the sky. Do you find yourself planning for your vacations more thoroughly than you do your retirement? It's not uncommon for Americans to spend more time planning our vacations than we spend planning our retirements. Maybe it's because planning a vacation is less stressful: Having a week at the beach go awry is, well, a walk on the beach compared to running out of money in retirement. Whatever the case, perhaps it would be better if you thought of your retirement as a vacation in and of itself—no clocking in, no boss, no overtime. If you felt unlimited by financial strain, what would you do?

We like to call this type of envisioning, "Planning Your Perfect Day!" It's an exercise we use with folks every day.

If you could plan out your absolutely perfect day, what would it look like? Take a moment and humor us here. If you could do anything, be anywhere, with anyone you wanted, for just one day, what would that look like? When would you wake up, what would you eat, where would you go, and how would you spend your time? What would you do for lunch, and what sights would you see? Who would be there with you enjoying this day? What would that evening look like? Would you watch the sunset over the ocean or maybe over the mountains? Would you have your favorite meal or bottle of wine while listening to your favorite music? When your head hit the pillow that night, would you be so thoroughly satisfied and excited to do it all over again the next day? That, my friend, is your Perfect Day! Our job is to help design and deliver as many of those days to you in retirement. To help you navigate how to use what you have to support where and what you want to accomplish! Part of that process is understanding our budget and where our dollars are currently going, so let's dive in.

Current Budget

A current expense report is one of the trickiest pieces of retirement spending. Many people assume the expenses of their lives in retirement will be different and, particularly, lower. After all, there will be no drive to work, no need for a formal wardrobe, and, perhaps most impactful of all, no more saving for retirement!

Yet, we often underestimate our daily spending habits. That's why I typically ask my clients to bring in their bank statements for the past year—they often reflect your *actual* spending, not just what you *think* you're spending.

I can't count the number of times I have sat with a couple, asked them about their spending, and had them give me a number that seemed incredibly low. When I ask them where the number came from, they usually say they estimated based off of their total bills. Yet, our spending is so much more than our mortgage, utilities, cable, phone, car, grocery, or credit card bills.

"What about clothes?" I ask, "Or dining out? What about gifts and coffees and last-minute birthday cards?" That's when the lights come on.

This is why I suggest collecting a year's worth of information. There is usually no such thing as a one-time purchase. Did you buy new furniture? Even if that is a rarity, do you think that will be the last time you *ever* buy furniture?

Another hefty expense is spending on the kids. Many of the couples I work with are quick to help their adult children, whether it's something like letting them live in the basement, paying for college, babysitting, paying an occasional bill, or contributing to a grandchild's college fund. Research concluded that 22 percent of adults receive some kind of financial support from parents. That segment jumps to almost 30 percent when factoring the generation we call millennials.[16]

My clients sometimes protest that what they do for their grown children can stop in retirement. They don't *need* to help. But I get it. Parents like to feel needed. And, while you never want to neglect saving for retirement in favor of taking on financial risks (like your child's student debt), the parents who help their adult children do so in part because it helps them feel fulfilled.

When it comes down to expenses, including (and especially) spending on your family, don't make your initial calculations based on what you *could* whittle your budget down to if you *had* to. Instead, start from where you are. Who wants to live off a bare-bones bank account in retirement?

Other Expenses

Once you have nailed down your current budget and your dreams or goals for retirement, there are a few other outstanding pieces to think about—some expenses many people don't take the time to consider before making and executing a plan. But I'm assuming you want to get it right, so let's take a look.

---

[16] Kamaron McNair. magnifymoney.com. October 26, 2021. "Nearly 30% of Millenials Still Receive Financial Support From Their Parents" https://www.magnifymoney.com/blog/news/parental-financial-support-survey/

Housing

Do you know where you want to live in retirement? This makes up a substantial piece of your income puzzle—since the typical American household owns a home, and it's generally their largest asset.

Some people prefer to live right where they are for as long as they can. Others have been waiting for retirement to pull the trigger on an ambitious move, like purchasing a new house, or even downsizing. Whatever your plans and whatever your reasons, there are quite a few things to consider.

Mortgage

Do you still have a mortgage? What may have been a nice tax boon in your working years could turn into a financial burden in your retirement. After all, when you are on a limited income, a mortgage is just one more bill sapping your financial strength. It is something to put some thought into whether you plan to age in place, move to your dream home, buy a house out of state, or live in a retirement community.

Upkeep and Taxes

A house without a mortgage still requires annual taxes. While it's tempting to think of this as a once-a-year expense, when you have limited earning potential, your annual tax bill might be something into which you put a little more forethought.

The costs of homeownership aren't just monetary. When you find yourself dealing with more house than you need, it can drain your time and energy. From keeping clutter at bay to keeping the lawn mower running, upkeep can be extensive and expensive. For some, that's a challenge they heartily accept and can comfortably take on. For others, the idea of yard work or cleaning an area larger than they need feels foolish.

For instance, Peggy discovered after her knee replacement that most of her house was inaccessible to her when she was laid up.

"It felt ridiculous to pay someone else to dust and vacuum a house I was only living in 40 percent of!"

Practicality and Adaptability

Erik and Magda are looking to retire within the next two decades. They just sold their old three-bedroom ranch-style house. Their twins are in high school, and the couple had wanted to "upgrade" for years. Now they live in a gorgeous 1940s three-story house with all the kitchen space they ever wanted, five sprawling bedrooms, and a library and media room for themselves and their children. Within months of moving in, the couple realized a house perfect for their active teens would no longer be perfect in five to fifteen years.

"We are already paying the mortgage for this house, but we've started saving for the next one," said Magda. "Because who wants to be going up two flights of stairs to their bedroom when they're seventy-eight?"

Others I know have encountered a similar situation in their personal lives. After a health crisis, one couple found the luxurious tub for two they slaved over installing had become a specter of a bad slip and safety risks. It's important to think through what your physical reality could be, whatever your long-term plan might be; and it's amazing how many people don't.

Contracts and Regulations

If you are looking into a cross-country move, be aware of new tax tables or local ordinances in the area where you are looking to move. After all, you don't want to experience sticker-shock when you are looking at downsizing or reducing your bills in retirement.

Along the same lines, if you are moving into a retirement community, be sure to look at the fine print. What happens if you must move into a different situation for long-term care? Will you be penalized? Will you be responsible for replacing your slot in the community? What are all of the fees, and what do they cover?

Inflation

As I write this in 2022, America has experienced a wave of inflation following a lengthy period of low inflation. Inflation zoomed to 8.5 percent in March 2022, a level not reached since 1981, and increased to 9.1 percent in June 2022.[17]

Core inflation is yet another measurement that excludes goods with prices that tend to be more volatile, such as food and energy costs. Core inflation for a 12-month period ending in April 2022 was 6.2 percent. It so happened energy prices rose a whopping 30.3 percent over that timeframe.[18]

---

[17] tradingeconomics.com. April 2022. "United States Inflation Rate." https://tradingeconomics.com/united-states/inflation-cpi
[18] U.S. Inflation Calculator. "United States Core Inflation Rates (1957-2022)"
https://www.usinflationcalculator.com/inflation/united-states-core-inflation-rates

However, inflation isn't a one-time bump; it has a cumulative effect. Again, that can impact the price of groceries greater than other goods. Even with relatively low inflation over the past few decades, an item you bought in 1997 for two dollars will cost $3.60 today.[19] Want to go to a show? A $20 ticket in 1997 would cost $40.34 in 2022.[20]

What if, in retirement, we hit a stretch like the late seventies and early eighties, when annual inflation rates of 10 percent became the norm? It may be wise to consider some extra padding in your retirement income plan to account for any potential increase in inflation in the future.

Aging

Also, in the expense category, think about longevity. We all hope to age gracefully. However, it's important to face the prospect of aging with a sense of realism.

The elephant in the room for many families is long-term care. No one wants to admit they will likely need it, but estimates indicate almost 70 percent of us could. [21] Aging is a significant piece of retirement income planning because you'll want to figure out how to set aside money for your care, either at home or away from it. The more comfortable you get with discussing

---

[19] Ibid.

[20] In2013dollars.com "Admission to movies, theaters, and concerts priced at $20 in 1997>$40.34 in 2022." https://www.in2013dollars.com/Admission-to-movies,-theaters,-and-concerts/price-inflation

[21] Moll Law Group. 2022. "The Cost of Long-Term Care." https://www.molllawgroup.com/the-cost-of-long-term-care.html

your wishes and plans with your loved ones, the easier planning for the financial side of it can be.

I discuss health care and potential long-term care costs in more detail elsewhere in this book, but, suffice it to say, nursing home care is expensive and typically not something you get to choose when you need.

It isn't just the costs of long-term care that pose a concern in living longer. It's also about covering the possible costs of everything else associated with living longer. For instance, if Henry retires from his job as a biochemical engineer at age sixty-five, perhaps he planned to have a very decent income for twenty years, until age eighty-five. But what if he lives until he's ninety-five? That's a whole third—ten years—more of personal income he will need.

Putting It All Together

Whew! So you have pulled together what you have, and you have a pretty good idea of where you want to be. Now your financial professional and you can go about the work of arranging what assets you have to cover what you need, as well as how you might try to cover any gaps you have.

Like the proverbial man in the Bible who built his house on a rock, I like to help my clients figure out how to cover their day-to-day living expenses—their needs—with insurance and other guaranteed income sources like pensions and Social Security.

No two retirements look identical. Everyone has different goals and dreams. However, just because our dreams differ, doesn't mean there is not an overall structure to retirement planning that can make each one of us successful.

Not too long ago, we were building a new home. We were so excited to have it built and see our vision become a reality. But the unpredictability of the Texas weather kept delaying the construction over and over again. As the saying goes, "If you don't like the weather in Texas, just wait fifteen minutes!"

The most important piece of our new home is (hopefully) the exact same as your current home. What is the most important part of your home? Well, in Texas it might be the air conditioner! In all seriousness, though, we all know it is the *foundation*. Nothing can happen without the builders forming a proper foundation. If the weather is too cold, the builders can't pour the cement. If it's too wet . . . they still can't pour. The conditions must be favorable for the foundation so all the other parts of the house are sturdily constructed. If there is a crack or the grade of the foundation is off, it can make a weak and compromised house.

Once you have a strong, solid foundation, then it seems like the building process moves at a lightning pace. The studs and walls go up. The inside begins to take shape. Finally, the roof is finished. Once everything is all put together properly, we are able to move in and start making memories. It's funny, because the foundation, walls, and roof are common in nearly every home. But no two homes are exactly identical. There are small to large differences that make each home unique, but the main structure is exactly the same! And, the more you live in it, the more it becomes unique because the décor and vibe start adopting your personality.

Your retirement is no different. As we discussed previously, we believe most people must have different buckets to support different things in retirement. The *foundation* of your retirement is centered around your *income* goals. No matter what your sit-on-the-porch number is, income (the blue bucket) is the foundation to your retirement house. Without proper income, nothing else can happen. No further construction can take place. You have to know, without a shadow of a doubt, that you will not run out of money. You must plan to live a really long time. Once that foundation is laid and in place, we can then start constructing the walls.

The walls are made up of your emergency fund (the green bucket). You need to know that, should something come up (i.e., an unexpected vacation opportunity or a repair on your car), with this bucket, you can have enough available money to tap into without disrupting your other accounts.

Lastly, the roof. The first thing on our new home that will have to be replaced when we get one of these Texas spring hail storms will be the roof. Well, when a financial "hail storm" hits, i.e., the market drops, the first thing that takes a beating is our market bucket (the red one). It's also the easiest one to fix and adjust.

So, think of your retirement plan like building a home. It needs to be structured with tried and true strategies and methods that work. It also needs to be customized enough to support your dreams and goals. That is what we believe and what we strive to deliver on every single day to everyone we serve!

Again, you should keep in mind there isn't one single financial vehicle, asset, or source that can fill all of your needs, and that's okay. One of the challenges of making a plan for your income in retirement is figuring out what products to use. You can let go of some of that stress when you accept the fact you will need a diverse portfolio—probably with bonds, stocks, insurance, and other income sources—not just one massive money pile.

One way to help shore up your income gaps is by working with your financial professional and a qualified tax advisor to mitigate your tax exposure. If you have a 401(k) or IRA, a financial advisor in your corner can help you figure out how and when to take distributions from your account in a way that ideally doesn't push you into a higher tax bracket. Or you might learn how to use tax-advantaged bonds more effectively. Effective tax planning isn't about just "adding" to your income. Especially concerning retirement, it's less about what you make than it is about what you keep. Paying a lower tax bill keeps more money in your pocket, which is where you want it when it comes to retirement income.

Now you can look at ways to cover your remaining retirement goals. Are there products like long-term care insurance that are specific to a certain kind of expense you anticipate? Is there a particular asset you want to use for your "play" money—money for trips and gifts for the grandkids? Is there any way you can portion off money for those charitable legacy plans?

Once you have analyzed your income wants, needs, and the realistic assets to cover them, you may have a gap. The masterstroke of a competent financial professional will be to help you figure out how you will cover that gap. Will you need to cut out a round of golf a week? Maybe skip the new car? Or will you need to take more significant action?

One way to cover an income gap is to consider working longer or even part time before retirement, even after that magical calendar date. This may not be the best "plan" for you; disabilities, work demands, and physical or emotional limitations can stymie the best-laid plans to continue working. However, if it is physically possible for you, this is one considerable way to help your assets last, for more than one reason.

In fact, 46 percent of the Americans responding to a survey report they plan to work part-time after retiring, while 18 percent indicated they planned to work past the age of seventy.[22]

When you're retired, you no longer have an employer paying you a steady check. It is up to you to make sure you have saved and planned for the income you need.

---

[22] Palash Ghosh. Forbes.com. May 6, 2021. "A Third Of Seniors Seek To Work Well Past Retirement Age, Or Won't Retire At All, Poll Finds"
https://www.forbes.com/sites/palashghosh/2021/05/06/a-third-of-seniors-seek-to-work-well-past-retirement-age-or-wont-retire-at-all-poll-finds/?sh=1d2ece836b95

CHAPTER 5

Social Security

Social Security is often the foundation piece of retirement income. Backed by the strength of the U.S. Treasury, it provides perhaps the most dependable paycheck you will have in retirement.

From the time you collect your first paycheck from whatever job made you a bonafide taxpayer (for me, it was flipping burgers at Burger Street), you are paying into the grand old Social Security system. What grew and developed out of the pressures of the Great Depression has become one of the most popular government programs in the country, and, if you pay in the equivalent of ten years or more, you, too, can benefit from the Social Security program.

Now, before we get into the nitty-gritty of Social Security, I'd like to address a current concern: Will Social Security still be there for you when you reach retirement age?

The Future of Social Security

This question is ever-present as headlines trumpet an underfunded Social Security program, alongside the flux of baby boomers who are retiring in droves, and the comparatively smaller younger generations who are bearing the responsibility of funding the system.

The Social Security Administration itself is a source of this concern as each Social Security statement now bears an asterisk that continues near the end of the summary:

> "*Your estimated benefits are based on current law. Congress has made changes to the law in the past and can do so at any time. The law governing benefit amounts may change because, by 2034, the payroll taxes collected will be enough to pay only about 79 percent of scheduled benefits."

Just a reminder, as if you needed one, that nothing in life is guaranteed.

Before you get too discouraged, though, here are a few thoughts to keep you going:

- Although those who retire after 2034 may only receive 79 cents on the dollar for their scheduled benefits, 79 percent is notably not zero.
- Social Security has made changes in the distant and near past to protect the fund's solvency, including increasing retirement ages and striking certain filing strategies.
- There are many changes Congress could make, and lawmakers are currently discussing how to fix the system, such as further increasing full retirement age and eligibility.
- One thing no one is seriously discussing? Reneging on current obligations to retirees or the soon-to-retire.

Take heart. The real answer to the question, "Will Social Security be there for me?" is still yes.

This question is important to consider when you look at how much we, as a nation, rely on this program. Did you know Social Security benefits replace about 40 percent of a person's original income when they retire?[23]

If you ask me, that's a pretty significant piece of your retirement income puzzle.

Another caveat? No one can legally "advise" you about your Social Security benefits.

"But, Scott," you may be thinking, "Isn't that part of what you do? And what about that nice gentleman at the Social Security Administration office I spoke with on the phone?"

Don't get me wrong. Social Security Administration employees know their stuff. They are trained to know policies and programs, and they are usually pretty quick to tell you what you can and cannot do. But the government specifically says that, because Social Security is a benefit you alone have paid into and earned, your Social Security decisions, too, are yours alone.

When it comes to financial professionals, we can't push you in any directions, either, BUT—there's a big but, here—working with a well-informed financial professional is still incredibly handy when it comes to your Social Security decisions. Why? Because someone who's worth his or her salt will know what withdrawal strategies might pertain to your specific situation, and

---

[23] ssa.gov. "Alternate Measure of Replacement Rates for Social Security Benefits and Retirement Income." https://www.ssa.gov/policy/docs/ssb/v68n2/v68n2p1.html

they will ask questions that can help you determine what you are looking for when it comes to your Social Security.

For instance, some people want the highest possible monthly benefit. Others want to start their benefits early, and not always because of financial need. I heard about one man who called in to start his Social Security payments the day he qualified, just because he liked to think of it as the government paying back a debt it owed him and he enjoyed the feeling of receiving a check from Uncle Sam.

Whatever your reasons, questions, or feelings regarding Social Security, the decision is yours alone; but working with a financial professional can help you put your options in perspective by showing you—both with industry knowledge and with proprietary software or planning processes—where your benefits fit into your overall strategy for retirement income.

One reason the federal government doesn't allow for "advice" related to Social Security, I suspect, is so no one can profit from giving you advice related to your Social Security benefit—or from providing any clarifications. Again, this is a sign of a good financial professional. Those who are passionate about their work will be knowledgeable about what benefit strategies might be to your advantage and will happily share those possible options with you.

Full Retirement Age

When it comes to Social Security, it seems like many people only think so far as "yes." They don't take the time to understand the various options available. Instead, because it is common knowledge you can begin your benefits at age sixty-two, that's what many of us do. While more people are opting to delay taking benefits, age sixty-two is still firmly the most popular age to start.[24]

What many people fail to understand is, by starting benefits early, they may be leaving a lot of money on the table. You see, the Social Security Administration bases your monthly benefit on two factors: your earnings history and your full retirement age (FRA).

From your earnings history, they pull the thirty-five years you made the most money and use a mathematical indexing formula to figure out a monthly average from those years. If you paid into the system for less than thirty-five years, then every year you didn't pay in will be counted as a zero.

Once they have calculated what your monthly earning would be at FRA, the government then calculates what to put on your check based on how close you are to FRA. FRA was originally set at sixty-five, but, as the population aged and lifespans lengthened, the government shifted FRA later and

---

24 Chris Kissell. moneytalknews.com. January 20, 2021. "This Is When the Most People Start Taking Social Security." https://www.moneytalksnews.com/the-most-popular-age-for-claiming-social-security/

later, based on an individual's year of birth. Check out the following chart to see when you will reach FRA.[25]

Age to Receive Full Social Security Benefits*	
(Called "full retirement age" or "normal retirement age.")	
Year of Birth*	FRA
1937 or earlier	65
1938	65 and 2 months
1939	65 and 4 months
1940	65 and 6 months
1941	65 and 8 months
1942	65 and 10 months
1943-1954	66
1955	66 and 2 months
1956	66 and 4 months
1957	66 and 6 months
1958	66 and 8 months
1959	66 and 10 months
1960 and later	67
If you were born on Jan. 1 of any year, you should refer to the previous year. (If you were born on the 1st of the month,	

[25] Social Security Administration. "Full Retirement Age." https://www.ssa.gov/planners/retire/retirechart.html

> *we figure your benefit (and your full retirement age) as if your birthday was in the previous month.)*

When you reach FRA, you are eligible to receive 100 percent of whatever the Social Security Administration says is your full monthly benefit.

Starting at age sixty-two, for every year before FRA you claim benefits, your monthly check is reduced by 5 percent or more. Conversely, for every year you delay taking benefits past FRA, your monthly benefit increases by 8 percent (until age seventy—after that, there is no monetary advantage to delaying Social Security benefits). While your circumstances and needs may vary, a lot of financial professionals still urge people to at least consider delaying until they reach age seventy.

Why wait?[26]

Taking benefits early could affect your monthly check by _____.								
62	63	64	65	FRA 66	67	68	69	70
-25%	-20%	-13.3%	-6.7%	0	+8%	+16%	+24%	+32%

My Social Security

As long as you are over age thirty, you have probably received a notice from the Social Security Administration telling you to activate something called My Social Security. This is a handy way to learn more about whatever your particular benefit options are, to

---

[26] Social Security Administration. April 2021. "Can You Take Your Benefits Before Full Retirement Age?"
https://www.ssa.gov/planners/retire/applying2.html

keep track of what your earnings record looks like, and to calculate the benefits you have accrued over the years.

Essentially, My Social Security is an online account you can activate to see what your personal Social Security picture looks like, which you can do at www.ssa.gov/myaccount. This can be extremely helpful when it comes to planning for income in retirement and figuring up the difference between your anticipated income versus anticipated expenses.

One other way My Social Security is helpful? It's a great way to see if there is a problem. For instance, I have heard of one woman who, through diligently checking her tax records against her Social Security profile, discovered her Social Security check was shortchanging her, based on her earnings history. After taking the discrepancy to the Social Security Administration, they sent her what they owed her in makeup benefits.

COLA

Social Security is a largely guaranteed piece of the retirement puzzle: If you get a statement that says to expect $1,000 a month, you can be sure you will get $1,000 a month. But there is one variable detail, and that is something called the cost-of-living adjustment, or COLA.

The COLA is an increase in your monthly check meant to address inflation in everyday life. After all, your expenses will likely continue to experience inflation in retirement, but you will no longer have the opportunity for raises, bonuses, or promotions you had when you were working. Instead, Social Security receives an annual cost-of-living increase tied to the Department of Labor's Consumer Price Index for Urban Wage Earners and Clerical Workers, or CPI-W. If the CPI-W measurement shows inflation rose a certain amount for regular goods and services, then Social Security recipients will see that reflected in their COLA.

The COLA averages 4 percent, but in a no- or low-inflation environment, such as in 2010, 2011, and 2016, Social Security recipients will not receive an adjustment. Some see the COLA as a perk, bump, or bonus, but, in reality, it works more like this: Your mom sends you to the store with $2.50 for a gallon of milk. Milk costs exactly $2.50. The next week, you go back with that same amount, but it is now $2.52 for a gallon, so you go back to Mom, and she gives you 2 cents. You aren't bringing home more milk—it just costs more money.

So the COLA is less about "making more money" and more about keeping seniors' purchasing power from eroding when inflation is a big factor, such as in 1975, when it was 8 percent![27] Still, don't let that detract from your enthusiasm about COLAs; after all, what if Mom's solution was: "Here's the same $2.50; try to find pennies from somewhere else to get that milk!"?

Spousal Benefits

We've talked about FRA, but another big Social Security decision concerns spousal benefits.

---

[27] Social Security Administration. "Cost-Of-Living Adjustment (COLA) Information for 2022." https://www.ssa.gov/cola/

If you or your spouse has a long stretch of zeros in your earnings history—perhaps if one of you stayed home for years, caring for children or sick relatives—you may want to consider filing for spousal benefits instead of filing on your own earnings history. A spousal benefit can be up to 50 percent of the primary wage earner's benefit at full retirement age.

To begin drawing a spousal benefit, you must be at least sixty-two years old, and the primary wage earner must have already filed for his or her benefit. While there are penalties for taking spousal benefits early (you could lose up to 67.5 percent of your check for filing at age sixty-two), you cannot earn credits for delaying past full retirement age.[28]

Like I wrote, the spousal benefit can be a big deal for those who don't have a very long pay history, but it's important to weigh your own earned benefits against the option of withdrawing based on a fraction of your spouse's benefits.

To look at how this could play out, let's use a hypothetical couple: Mary Jane, who is sixty, and Peter, who is sixty-two.

Let's say Peter's benefit at FRA, in his case sixty-six, would be $1,600. If Peter begins his benefits right now, four years before FRA, his monthly check will be $1,200. If Mary Jane begins taking spousal benefits in two years at the earliest date possible, her monthly benefits will be reduced by 67.5 percent, to $520 per month (remember, at FRA, the most she can qualify for is half of Peter's FRA benefit).

---

[28] Social Security Administration. "Retirement Planner: Benefits For You As A Spouse."
https://www.ssa.gov/planners/retire/applying6.html

What if Peter and Mary Jane both wait until FRA? At sixty-six, Peter begins taking his full benefit of $1,600 a month. Two years later, when she reaches age sixty-six, Mary Jane will qualify for $800 a month. By waiting until FRA, the couple's monthly benefit goes from $1,720 to $2,400.

What if Peter delays until age seventy to get his maximum possible benefit? For each year past FRA he delays, his monthly benefits increase by 8 percent. This means, at seventy, he could file for a monthly benefit of $2,176. However, delayed retirement credits do not affect spousal benefits, so as soon as Peter files at seventy, Mary Jane would also file (at age sixty-eight) for her maximum benefit of $800, so their highest possible combined monthly check is $2,976.[29]

When it comes to your Social Security benefits, you obviously will want to consider if a monthly check based on a fraction of your spouse's earnings will be comparable to or larger than your own earnings history.

I've thrown a lot of numbers at you to consider, like your FRA based on your year of birth, as well as COLA and spousal benefits (and we haven't even gotten to taxes!), but here's another date to think about: Jan. 2, 1954. What's important about that, you ask? For those born on or after that date, you can only make the choice to withdraw your benefits one way, one time. That means you will have to pick whether to take a spousal benefit or use your own earnings history, and whichever one you choose will be the check you get every month for the duration of your retirement.

_____

[29] Office of the Chief Actuary. Social Security Administration. "Social Security Benefits: Benefits for Spouses."

However, if you were born BEFORE Jan. 2, 1954, read on.

If you were born before Jan. 2, 1954, you are eligible to change your benefit withdrawal strategy *even after you have begun withdrawals.* This means that you could begin taking a spousal benefit at age sixty-two or FRA while allowing the benefits based on your own earnings history to accrue.[30]

Let's look back to Mary Jane and Peter to see how this could theoretically work. We know that if they both file at FRA, Mary Jane will receive $800 a month on top of Peter's $1,600 benefit when she files. But what if her own earned credit at FRA was $700? In four years, when Mary Jane turns seventy, the monthly benefit based on her personal earnings will have grown from $700 to $924. At seventy, she could file to trade up her $800 monthly spousal benefit for a $924 monthly check. Remember, this only works for Mary Jane if she was born before Jan. 2, 1954.

Divorced Spouses

There are a few considerations for those of us who have gone through a divorce. If you 1) were married for ten years or more *and* 2) have since been divorced for at least two years *and* 3) are unmarried *and* 4) your ex-spouse qualifies to begin Social Security, you qualify for a spousal benefit based on your ex-husband or ex-wife's earnings history at FRA. A divorced spousal benefit is different from the married spousal benefit in

---

[30] Social Security Administration. "Retirement Planner: Benefits For Your Spouse."
https://www.ssa.gov/planners/retire/applying6.html

one way: You don't have to wait for your ex-spouse to file before you can file yourself.[31]

For instance, Charles and Moira were married for fifteen years before their divorce, when he was thirty-six and she was forty. Moira has been remarried for twenty years, and, although Charles briefly remarried, his second marriage ended after a few years. Charles' benefits are largely calculated based on his many years of volunteering in schools, meaning his personal monthly benefit is close to zero.

Although Moira has deferred her retirement, opting to delay benefits until she is seventy, Charles can begin taking benefits calculated off of Moira's work history at FRA as early as sixty-two. However, he will also have the option of waiting until FRA to collect the maximum, or 50 percent of Moira's earned monthly benefit at her FRA.

Widowed Spouses

If your marriage ended with the death of your spouse, you might claim a benefit for your spouse's earned income as his or her widow/widower, called a survivor's benefit. Unlike a spousal benefit or divorced benefits, if your husband or wife dies, you are allowed to claim his or her full benefit. Also, unlike spousal benefits, if you need to, you can begin taking income when you turn sixty. However, as with other benefit options, your monthly check will be permanently reduced for withdrawing benefits before FRA.

---

[31] Social Security Administration. "Retirement Planner: If You Are Divorced."
https://www.ssa.gov/planners/retire/divspouse.html

If your spouse began taking benefits before he or she died, you can't delay withdrawing your survivor's benefits to get delayed credits. The Social Security Administration maintains you can only get as much from a survivor's benefit as your deceased spouse might have received, had he or she lived.[32]

Taxes, Taxes, Taxes

With Social Security, as with everything, it is important to consider taxes. It may be surprising, but your Social Security benefits are not tax-free. Despite having been taxed to accrue those benefits in the first place, you may have to pay Uncle Sam income taxes on up to 85 percent of your Social Security.

The way the Social Security Administration figures these taxes is what they call the provisional income formula. Your provisional income formula differs from the adjusted gross income you use for your regular income taxes. Instead, to find out how much of your Social Security benefit is taxable, the Social Security Administration calculates it this way:

Provisional Income = Adjusted Gross Income + Nontaxable Interest + ½ of Social Security

See that piece about nontaxable interest? That generally means interest from government bonds and notes. It surprises many people that, although you may not pay taxes on those assets, their income will count against you when it comes to Social Security taxation.

---

[32] Social Security Administration. "Social Security Benefit Amounts For The Surviving Spouse By Year Of Birth." https://www.ssa.gov/planners/survivors/survivorchartred.html

Once you have figured out your provisional income (also called "combined income"), you can use the following chart to figure out your Social Security taxes.[33]

Taxes on Social Security		
Provisional Income = Adjusted Gross Income + Nontaxable Interest + ½ of Social Security		
If you are ____ and your provisional income is____, then...		Uncle Sam will tax ___ of your Social Security
Single	Married, filing jointly	
Less than $25,000	Less than $32,000	0%
$25,000 to $34,000	$32,000 to $44,000	Up to 50%
More than $34,000	More than $44,000	Up to 85%

This is one more reason it may be to your advantage to work with a financial and tax professional: They can look at your entire financial picture to help make your overall retirement approach as tax-efficient as possible—including your Social Security benefit.

One of the main ways to consider making your Social Security benefits tax-efficient is to make your provisional income as low as possible. If you have saved most of your money in the tax-deferred accounts,

---

[33] Social Security Administration. "Benefits Planner: Income Taxes and Your Social Security Benefits." https://www.ssa.gov/planners/taxes.html

then you know at age seventy-two you will be required to withdraw money whether you want to or not. The goal would be to adjust the balance in these accounts low enough so, at age seventy-two, the amount you have to withdraw each year is lower than the standard deduction you take on your tax return. That way the standard deduction off-sets this income, and your provisional income stays low, thus, potentially relieving the taxation of your Social Security payments.

We hope one takeaway from this chapter is just how complicated Social Security planning can be. In our office, we call it a "beast unto itself!" For many it will be the largest "retirement account" they own. The decisions we make on when and how to claim it can add up to thousands of dollars throughout our lifetime, so it deserves proper attention and planning. We can take advantage of numerous strategies to help ensure we are maximizing our benefits. If you are not sure when to claim and especially how to coordinate it with your other retirement income, then please seek us out. You only get one shot at claiming your benefit, and we want to be certain you are receiving the most you can. After all, this is your hard-earned money! You paid into the system, so let's make sure we aren't leaving any money behind!

Working and Social Security: The Earnings Test

If you haven't reached FRA, but you started your Social Security benefits and are still working, things get a little hairy.

Because you have started Social Security payments, the Social Security Administration will pay out your benefits (at that reduced rate, of course, because you haven't reached your FRA). Yet, because you are working, the organization must also withhold from your check to add to your benefits, which you are already collecting. See how this complicates matters?

To straighten the situation, the government has what is called the earnings test. For 2022, you can earn up to $19,560 without it affecting your Social Security check. But for every $2 you earn past that amount, the Social Security Administration will withhold $1. The earnings test loosens in the year of your FRA; if you are reaching FRA in 2022, you can earn up to $51,960 before you run into the earnings test, and the government only withholds $1 for every $3 past that amount. The month you will reach FRA, you are no longer subject to any earnings withholding. For instance, if you are still working and will turn sixty-six on December 28, 2022, you would only have to worry about the earnings test until December, and then you can ignore it entirely. Keep in mind, the money the government withholds from your Social Security benefits while you are working before FRA will be tacked back onto your benefits check after FRA.[34]

---

[34] Social Security Administration. "Exempt Amounts Under the Earnings Test." https://www.ssa.gov/oact/cola/rtea.html

CHAPTER 6

401(k)s & IRAs

H ave you heard? Today's retirement is not your
dad's retirement. You see, back in the day, it
was pretty common to work for one company
for the vast majority of your career and then retire with
a gold watch and a pension.

The gold watch was a symbol of the quality time you
put in at that company, but the pension was more than
a symbol. Instead, it was a guarantee—as solid as your
employer—that they would repay your hard work with
a certain amount of income in your old age. Did you see
the caveat there? Your pension's guarantee was *as solid
as your employer*. The problem was, what if your
employer went under?

Companies that failed couldn't pay their retired
employees' pensions, leading to financial challenges
for many. Beginning in 1974 with Congress' passage of
the Employee Retirement Income Security Act, federal
legislation and regulations aimed at protecting retirees
were everywhere, including a relatively obscure section
of the Internal Revenue Code, added in 1978. Section
401(k), to be specific.

IRC section 401, subsection k, created tax
advantages for employer-sponsored financial

products, even if the main contributor was the employee him or herself. Over the years, more employers took note, beginning an age of transition away from pensions and toward 401(k) plans. A 401(k) is a retirement account with certain tax benefits and restrictions on the investments or other financial products used inside of it.

Essentially, 401(k)s and their individual retirement account (IRA) counterparts are "wrappers" that provide tax benefits around other assets; typically, the assets that compose IRAs and 401(k)s are mutual funds, stock and bond mixes, and money market accounts. However, IRA and 401(k) contents are becoming more diverse these days, with some companies offering different kinds of annuity options within their plans.

Where pensions are defined-*benefit* plans, 401(k)s and their individual retirement account (IRA) counterparts are defined-*contribution* plans. The one-word change outlines the basic difference. Pensions spell out what you can expect to receive from the plan but not necessarily how much money it will take to fund those benefits. With 401(k)s, an employer sets a standard for how much they will contribute (if any), and you can be certain of what you are contributing, but there is no outline for what you can expect to receive in return for those contributions.

Modern employment looks very different. A 2020 survey by the Bureau of Labor Statistics determined U.S. workers stayed with their employers a median of 4.1 years. Workers ages fifty-five to sixty-four had a little more staying power and were most likely to stay with their employer for about ten years.[35] Participation in 401(k) plans has steadily risen this century, totaling $7.3 trillion in assets in 2021 compared to $3.1 trillion in 2011. About 60 million active participants engaged in 401(k) plans in 2020.[36]

Those statistics make it clear that 401(k) plans have replaced pensions at many companies and, for that matter, a gold watch.

My grandfather was born in the early 1920s. He was one of eight children and a first-generation American. My great-grandparents came over to this country from Italy. Like most men born in the early 1920s, my grandfather was drafted into World War II. He was drafted into the US Army Air Corps, what we today call the Air Force.

After going through the assessments and boot camp, he was assigned the position of bombardier. If you don't know what a bombardier is, it's the member of the flight crew who looks through the telescope to make sure they are over the proper target. He then lifts a switch, presses a button and says, "Bombs away!"

Some of my earliest memories of my grandfather are of being in his living room and seeing him sitting in his big Lay-Z-Boy recliner. I would climb up in his lap, and he would recline it all the way back. My head would rest on his soft, flannel button-up shirt, and I would breathe

---

[35] Bureau of Labor Statistics. September 22, 2020. "Employee Tenure Summary."
https://www.bls.gov/news.release/tenure.nr0.htm

[36] Investment Company Institute. October 11, 2021. "Frequently Asked Questions About 401(k) Plan Research."
https://www.ici.org/faqs/faq/401k/faqs_401k#:~:text=In%202 020%2C%20there%20were%20about,of%20former%20employe es%20and%20retirees

in his cologne as he told story after story. He'd reminisce over the twenty-three successful missions he flew over Europe in the war as I hung on every word. Not too long before he passed away at the age of ninety, he actually gave me the wings he earned serving our country during WWII. They are one of my most prized possessions.

When the war ended and he met my grandmother, they settled in a small town in New Jersey and began a family. He wasn't sure what he wanted to do to support this new family, but he knew he loved people and serving others. So, he decided to become the town's local butcher. I found out at his funeral that, because he was so meticulous and so precise in his carving of the meat, the town nicknamed him "The Surgeon." Can you believe that? What an incredible nickname if you're a butcher!

On one of his last trips down to visit us in Texas, we were at his favorite lunch spot, Chick-fil-A. We spent most of that afternoon talking about my business and company. He thought it was the neatest thing in the world that I was an entrepreneur and business owner.

When there was a break in the conversation, I asked my grandfather, "How did you know you were able to retire? How did you know you had enough money and you weren't going to run out? How did you know it was just all going to be okay?"

He thought for a moment and then said to me, "Scott, you know I was a butcher for all those years. Well, I also was a member of two different unions. So, when I decided to retire, I went in a week before and told them I was all done. The next week they threw me and your grandmother a party. It was great. All of our friends and family were there. They called me up and one union presented me with a gold watch. The other gave me a new car. But to answer your question, how did I know I was ready? It is because each of those unions also gave me and your grandmother a pension we still collect today, and that money is on top of our Social Security."

I remember thinking, "Wow, what a great deal."

He continued, "You remember when your grandmother got sick and spent all those months in the hospital?"

"Yessir, I do," I said.

"Did you know I never received a bill for her care? That's because those unions also gave us full health care and long-term care benefits above and beyond what Medicare covers!"

The lunch ended that day, and I dropped my grandfather off. As I made my way back to the office, I couldn't stop thinking about his story. It dawned on me that my grandfather had what I call a *"Turn-Key Retirement."* He had guaranteed income that showed up like clockwork each month. He could never outlive this income, and it wouldn't fluctuate based on the stock market. The kids were grown, and the house was paid off. He and my grandmother could plan their life around this. Their health care was covered. All the risk and thinking were taken away from them. They were able to just enjoy retirement without worry.

Those were the good old days. Retirement is completely different today. You and I didn't get a Turn-Key Retirement. No . . . what you and I have is the "Do-It-Yourself Retirement." We've got to figure out what to do when taxes go up and the market goes down. We have to make a plan for how we are going to pay for our healthcare and long-term care. We better make sure we have enough income to last our lifetime, and that it is not dependent on the stock market fluctuating up or down. We have to take care of it all on our own!

If there is anything to learn from this paradigm shift, it's that you have to look out for you. Whether you have worked for a company for two years or twenty, you are still the one who has to look out for your own best interests. That holds doubly true when it comes to preparing for retirement. If you are one of the lucky ones who still has a pension, good for you. But for the rest of us, it is likely that a 401(k)—or possibly one of its nonprofit or government-sector counterparts, a 403(b) or 457 plan—is one of your biggest assets for retirement.

Some employers offer incentives to contribute to their company plans, like a company match. On that subject, I have one thing to say: *do it*! Nothing in life is free, as they say, but a company match on your retirement funds is about as close to free money as I think it gets. If you can make the minimum to qualify for your company's match at all, go for it.

Now, it's likely that, during our working years, we mostly "set and forget" our 401(k) funding. Because it is tax-advantaged, your employer is taking money from your paycheck—before taxes—and putting it into your plan for you. Maybe you got to pick a selection of investments, or maybe your company only offers one choice of investment in your 401(k). Either way, while you are gainfully employed, your most impactful decision may just be the decision to continue funding your plan in the first place. But when you are ready to retire or move jobs, you have choices to make that require a little more thought and care.

When you are ready to part ways with your job, you have a few options:

- Leave the money where it is
- Take the cash (and pay income taxes and perhaps a 10 percent additional federal tax if you are younger than age fifty-nine-and-one-half)
- Transfer the money to another employer plan (if the new plan allows)
- Roll the money over into a self-directed IRA

Now, these are just general options. You will have to decide, hopefully with the help of a financial professional, what's right for you. For instance, 401(k)s are typically pretty closely tied to the companies that offer them, so when changing jobs, it may not always be possible to transfer a 401(k) to another 401(k). Leaving the money where it is may also be out of the question—some companies have direct cash-out or rollover policies once someone is no longer employed.

Remember what we said earlier about how we change jobs more often these days? That means you likely have a 401(k) with your current company, but you may also have a string of IRAs trailing you from other jobs.

We have a philosophy for this situation. If you aren't at your old job, then your money shouldn't be, either! Far too often people leave jobs or change careers and leave their money at the previous employer. Maybe it's a lot of money, or maybe it's a little. The dollar amount is insignificant, but you worked hard and earned it, and you need to keep an eye on it. Every little bit makes a difference.

Part of our process is to visually draw out each account you own. Every account has its own box on the page. Many people are so surprised when they see just how many boxes (accounts) they actually have. Keeping up with each individual account can be cumbersome. While you are working and saving, you get to make decisions in silos. When you make a decision on one account, it typically only affects that account. However, when you retire and start spending, all the accounts become "connected." This means the way you withdraw money from your IRA/401(k) will not only affect that account but also potentially impact your Social Security taxation and Medicare premiums. It is imperative to make sure accounts are consolidated and goals are defined as we withdraw money.

When it comes to your retirement income, it's important to be able to pull together ALL of your assets, so you can examine what you have and where.

Tax-Qualified, Tax-Preferred, Tax-Deferred ... Still TAXED

Financial media often cite IRAs and 401(k)s for their tax benefits. After all, with traditional plans, you put your money in, pre-tax, and it hopefully grows for years, even decades, untaxed. That's why these accounts are called tax-qualified or tax-deferred assets. They aren't TAX-FREE! Rarely does Uncle Sam allow business to continue without receiving his piece of the pie, and your retirement assets are no different. If you didn't pay taxes on the front end, you will pay taxes on the money you withdraw from these accounts in retirement. Don't get me wrong: This isn't an inherently bad thing, nor is it a good thing; it's just the way it is. It's important to understand, though, for the sake of planning ahead.

In retirement, many people assume they will be in a lower tax bracket. Are you planning to pare down your lifestyle in retirement? Perhaps you are, and perhaps you will have substantially less income in retirement. But many of my clients tell me they want to live life more or less the same as they always have. The money they would previously have spent on business attire or gas for their commute they now want to spend on hobbies and grandchildren. That's all fine, and for many of them, it is doable, but does it put them in a lower tax bracket? Probably not.

Keep in mind, IRAs, 401(k)s, and their alternatives have a few limitations because of their special tax status. For one thing, the IRS sets limits on your contributions to these retirement accounts. If you are contributing to a 401(k) or an equivalent nonprofit or government plan, your annual contribution limit is $20,500 (as of 2022). If you are fifty or older, the IRS allows additional contributions, called "catch-up contributions," of up to $6,500 on top of the regular limit of $20,500.[37] For an IRA, the limit is $7,000, with a catch-up limit of an additional $1,000.[38]

Because their tax advantages come from their intended use as retirement income, withdrawing funds from these accounts before you turn fifty-nine-and-

---

[37] Jackie Stewart. Kiplinger.com. December 17, 2021. "401(k) Contribution Limits for 2022."
https://www.kiplinger.com/retirement/retirement-plans/401ks/603949/401k-contribution-limits-for-2022
[38] Fidelity.com. 2021."IRA contribution limits."
https://www.fidelity.com/retirement-ira/contribution-limits-deadlines

one-half can carry stiff penalties. In addition to fees your investment management company might charge, you will have to pay income tax *and* a 10 percent federal tax penalty.

Because their tax advantages come from their intended use as retirement income, withdrawing funds from these accounts before you turn fifty-nine-and-one-half can carry stiff penalties. In addition to fees your investment management company might charge, you will have to pay income tax *and* a 10 percent federal tax penalty, with few exceptions.

The fifty-nine-and-one-half rule for retirement accounts is incredibly important to remember, especially when you're young. Younger workers are often tempted to cash out an IRA from a previous employer and then are surprised to find their checks missing 20 percent of the account value to income taxes, penalty taxes, and account fees.

Many millennials I see in my practice say, while they may be socking money away in their workplace retirement plan, it is often the *only* place they are saving. This could be problematic later because of the fifty-nine-and-one-half rule; what if you have an emergency? It is important to fund your retirement, but you need to have some liquid assets handy as emergency funds. This can help you avoid breaking into your retirement accounts and incurring taxes and penalties because of the fifty-nine-and-one-half rule.

RMDs

Remember how we talked about the 401(k) or IRA being a "tax wrapper" for your funds? Well, eventually, Uncle Sam will want a bite of that candy bar. So, another condition of these accounts is that, beginning at seventy-two, the government requires you withdraw a portion of your account, which they calculate based on the size of your account and your estimated lifespan. This required minimum distribution—or RMD—is the government's insurance that they will at some point collect taxes from your earnings. Because you didn't pay taxes on the front end, you will now pay income taxes on whatever you withdraw, including your RMDs. *Also*, let me just remind you not to play chicken with the U.S. government; if you don't take your RMDs starting at seventy-two, you will have to write a check to the IRS for 50 *percent* of the amount of your missed RMDs.

Roth

Since the Taxpayer Relief Act of 1997, there has been a different kind of retirement account, or "tax wrapper," available to the public: the Roth. Roth IRAs and Roth 401(k)s each differ from their traditional counterparts in one big way: You pay your taxes on the front end. This means once your post-tax money is in the Roth account, as long as you follow the rules and limitations of that account, your distributions are truly tax-free. You won't pay income tax when you take withdrawals, so, in turn, you don't have to worry about RMDs.

As previously mentioned, taxes are one of the main variables we can manipulate and control in our retirement. While we don't set the tax rates—Congress does that—we do control our income. Roth IRAs can be a tremendous vehicle to use for generating tax-free money later on. If you believe taxes are going to rise over the course of your lifetime, you should take a long look at this tool. It might be an excellent vehicle to help shelter yourself from future taxation.

Taking Charge

As mentioned earlier, the 401(k) and IRA have largely replaced pensions, but they aren't an equal trade.

Pensions are employer-funded; the money feeding into them is money that wouldn't ever show up on your pay stub. Because 401(k)s are self-funded, you must actively and consciously save. This distinction has made a difference when it comes to funding retirement. The average 401(k) balance for a person age sixty to sixty-nine is $195,500, but the median likely tells the full story. The median 401(k) balance for a person age sixty to sixty-nine is $62,000. A general suggestion derived from those statistics is to aim, by age thirty, to have saved an amount equal to 50 to 100 percent of your annual salary.[39] For some thirty-year-olds, saving half an annual salary by age thirty is more than some sixty-to-sixty-nine-year-olds have saved for their entire lives.

---

[39] Arielle O'Shea. Nerd Wallet. March 17, 2021. "The Average 401(k) Balance by Age."
https://www.nerdwallet.com/article/investing/the-average-401k-balance-by-age

There can be many reasons why people underfund their retirement plans, like being overwhelmed by the investment choices or taking withdrawals from IRAs when they leave an employer, but the reason at the top of the list is this: People simply aren't participating to begin with.

So, whether you have a 401(k) with an employer or use an IRA alternative with a private company, separate from your workplace, the most important retirement savings decision you can make is to sock away your money somewhere in the first place.

CHAPTER 7

Estate & Legacy

I n my practice, I devote a significant portion of my time to matters of estates. That doesn't mean drawing up wills or trusts or putting together powers of attorney or anything like that. After all, I'm not an estate planning attorney. But I am a financial professional, and what part of the "estate" isn't affected by money matters?

I've included this chapter because I have seen people do it wrong. Clients, or clients' families, have come in after experiencing a death in the family and have found themselves in the middle of probate, high taxes, or a discovery that something unforeseen (often long-term care) drained the estate.

Alternately, I have seen people do it right: clients or families who visit my office to talk about legacies and how to make them last, adult children who have room to grieve without an added burden of unintended costs, without stress from a family ruptured because of inadequate planning.

I will share some of those stories here, not to give specific advice (obviously you have unique circumstances and will need the help of an attorney to be sure your wishes are carried out), but to give you some things to think about and to underscore the importance of planning ahead.

You Can't Take It With You

When it comes to legacy and estate planning, the most important thing is to *do it*. I have heard people from clients to celebrities (rap artist Snoop Dogg comes to mind) say they aren't interested in what happens to their assets when they die because they'll be dead. That's certainly one way to look at it. But I think that's a very selfish way to go about things—we all have people and causes we care about, not to mention those who care about us. Even if the people we love don't *need* what we leave behind, they can still be fined or legally tied up in the probate process or burial costs if we don't plan for those. And that's not even considering what happens if you become incapacitated at some point while you are still alive. Having a plan in place can greatly reduce the stress of those responsibilities on your loved ones; it's just a loving thing to do.

Documents

There are a few documents that lay the groundwork of legacy planning. You've probably heard of all or most of them, but I'd like to review what they are and how people commonly use them. These are all things you should talk about with an estate planning attorney to establish your legacy.

Powers of Attorney

A power of attorney, or POA, is a document that gives someone the authority to act on your behalf and in your best interests. These come in handy in situations where you cannot be present (think vacation where you get stuck in Canada) or, for durable powers of attorney, even when you are incapacitated (think in a coma or coping with dementia).

It is important to have powers of attorney in place and to appoint someone you trust to act on your behalf in these matters. Have you ever heard of someone who was incapacitated after a car accident, whether from head trauma or being in a coma for weeks—sometimes months? Do you think their bills stopped coming due during that time? I like my phone company and my bank, but neither one is about to put a moratorium on sending me bills, particularly not for an extended and interminable period. A power of attorney would have the authority to make sure your mortgage gets paid or cancel your cable while you are unable.

You can have multiple POAs and require them to act jointly.

What this looks like: Do you think two heads are better than one? One man, Chris, relied significantly on his two sons' opinions for both his business and personal matters. He appointed both sons as joint POA, requiring both their signoffs for his medical and financial matters.

You can have multiple POAs who can act independently.

What this looks like: Irene had three children with whom she routinely stayed. They lived in different areas of the country, which she thought was an advantage; one month she might be hiking out West, the next she could enjoy the newest off-Broadway production, and the next she could soak up some Southern sun. She named her three children as independently authorized POAs so, if something happened, no matter where she was, the child closest could step in to act on her behalf.

You can have POAs who have different responsibilities.

What this looks like: Although Luke's friend Claire, a nurse, was his go-to and POA for health-related issues, financial matters usually made her nervous, so he appointed his good neighbor, Matt, as his POA in all of his financial and legal matters.

In addition to POAs, it may be helpful to have an advanced medical directive. This is a document where you have pre-decided what choices you would make about different health scenarios. An advanced medical directive can help ease the burden for your medical POA and loved ones, particularly when it comes to end-of-life care.

Doug has been a long-term client of ours. He has an older brother, Gary. They all lived close to each other so they could take care of their ailing mother.

During one of his reviews, Doug confided his mother wasn't doing well and was in hospice care. Given her health situation, there were some treatments they could provide her to extend her life just a little. Doug thought it was best not to pursue the treatments and let his mother transition to end-of-life care. However, Gary wanted to start a few of the treatments and keep their mom here for as long as possible. It was clear Doug and his brother were at odds as to the proper course of action. When we asked Doug what his mom had laid out in her medical directive, he said she didn't have one. She wasn't in a state to make this type of decision anymore, and it was evident a wedge was forming between the two brothers. Ultimately, Doug and Gary decided it was best to let Mom go.

So much of the emotion and hard feelings could have been avoided with just a little planning. If a few documents were in place, Doug and Gary could have spent more time caring for Mom and less time debating what she would have wanted if she would have stated her intentions within her estate planning documents. Have you planned this out? Do your children know what your wishes are? Does your spouse know?

All too often, folks forget about having a POA and medical directives. These documents are so vital. The last thing you want is to have the hospital or a loved one having to make a decision that is not in alignment with your wishes.

Wills

Perhaps the most basic document of legacy planning, a will is a legal document wherein you outline your wishes for your estate. When it comes to your estate after your death, having a will is the foundation of your legacy. Without one, your loved ones are left behind, guessing what you would have wanted, and the court will largely split your assets according to whatever the state's defaults are. And maybe that's exactly what you wanted, as far as anyone knows, right? Because even if you told your nephew he could have your car he's been driving, if it's not in writing, it still might go to the brother, sister, son, or daughter to whom you aren't talking.

However, it may not be enough just to have a will. Even with a will, your assets will be subject to probate. Probate is what we call the state's process for determining a will's validity. A judge will go through your will to question if it is in conflict with state law, if it is the most up-to-date document, if you were mentally competent at the time it was in order, etc. For some, this is a quick, easily resolved process. For others, particularly if someone steps forward to contest the will, it may take years to settle, all the while subjecting the assets to court costs and attorney's fees.

One other undesirable piece of the probate process is that it is a public process. That means anyone can go to the courthouse, ask for copies of the case, and find out your assets, as well as who is slated to receive what and who is disputing.

It's also important to remember beneficiary lines trump wills. So, that large life insurance policy? What if, when you bought it fifteen years ago, you wrote your ex-husband's name on the beneficiary line? Even if you stipulate otherwise in your will, the company holding your policy will pay out to your ex-spouse. Or, how about the thousands of dollars in your IRA you dedicated to your "children" thirty years ago, but one of your children was killed in a car accident, leaving his wife and two toddlers behind? That IRA is going to transfer to your remaining children, with nothing for your daughter-in-law and grandchildren.

That may paint a grim portrait, but I can't underscore enough the importance of working with a skilled estate planning attorney, for the sake of your loved ones, to keep your will and beneficiary lines up to date as your life changes.

Trusts

Another piece of legacy planning to consider is the trust.

A trust is set up through an attorney and allows a third party, or trustee, to hold your assets and determine how they will pass to your beneficiaries. Many people are skeptical of trusts because they assume trusts are only appropriate for the fabulously wealthy.

However, a simple trust will likely cost more than $1,000 if prepared by an attorney and fees can be higher for couples.[40] But a trust can help you avoid both the expense and publicity of probate, provide a more immediate transfer of wealth, avoid some taxes, and provide you greater control over your legacy.

For instance, if you want to set aside some funds for a grandchild's college education, you can make it a requirement he or she enrolls in classes before your trust will dispense any funds. Like a will, beneficiary lines will override your trust conditions, so you must still keep insurance policies and other assets up to date.

Like any financial or legal consideration, there are many options these days beyond the "yes/no" of having a trust. For one thing, you will need to consider if you

---

[40] Rickie Houston. smartasset.com. "How Much Does It Cost to Set Up a Trust? https://smartasset.com/estate-planning/how-much-does-it-cost-to-set-up-a-trust

want your trust to be revocable (you can change the terms while you are alive) or irrevocable (can't be changed; you are no longer the "owner" of the contents). A brief note here about irrevocable trusts: While they have significant and greater tax benefits, they are still subject to a Medicaid look-back period. This means, if you transfer your assets into an irrevocable trust in an attempt to shelter them from a Medicaid spend-down, you will be ineligible for Medicaid coverage of long-term care for five years. Yet, an irrevocable trust can avoid both probate and estate taxes, and it can even protect assets from legal judgments against you.

Another thing to remember when it comes to trusts, in general, is that, even if you have set up a trust, you must remember to fund it. In my eleven years of financial work, I've had numerous clients come to me, assuming they have protected their assets with a trust. When we talk about taxes and other pieces of their legacy, it turns out they never retitled any assets or changed any paperwork on the assets they wanted in the trust. So please remember, a trust is just a bunch of fancy legal papers if you haven't followed through on retitling your assets.

Taxes

Although charitable contributions, trusts, and other tax-efficient strategies can reduce your tax bill, it's unlikely your estate will be passed on entirely tax-free. Yet, when it comes to building a legacy that can last for generations, taxes can be one of the biggest drains on the impact of your hard work.

For 2020, the federal estate exemption was $11.58 million per individual and $23.16 million for a married couple, with estates facing up to a 40 percent tax rate after that. In 2022, those limits increased to $12.06 million for individuals and $24.12 million for married couples, with the 40 percent top level gift and estate tax remaining the same. Currently, the new estate limits are set to increase with inflation until January 1, 2026, when they will "sunset" back to the inflation-adjusted 2017 limits.[41] And that's not taking into account the various state regulations and taxes regarding estate and inheritance transfers.

One "frequent flyer" on the tax concern list: retirement accounts.

Your IRA or 401(k) can be a source of tax issues when you pass away. For one thing, taking funds from a sizeable account can trigger a large tax bill. However, if you leave the assets in the account, there are still required minimum distributions (RMDs), which will take effect even after you die. If you pass the account to your spouse, he or she can keep taking your RMDs as is, or your spouse can retitle the account in his or her name and receive RMDs based on his or her life expectancy. Remember, if you don't take your RMDs, the IRS will take up to 50 percent of whatever your required distribution was, plus you will still have to pay income taxes whenever you withdraw that money. Thanks to rules inacted in 2020, anyone who inherits your IRA with few exceptions (your spouse, a beneficiary less than ten years younger, a disabled

---

[41] Rocky Mengle. Kiplinger. November 10, 2021. "Estate Tax Exemption Amount Goes Up for 2022." https://www.kiplinger.com/taxes/601639/estate-tax-exemption-2022

adult child, to name a few) will need to empty the account within ten years of your death.

Also—and this is a pretty big also—check with an attorney if you are considering putting your IRA or 401(k) in a trust. An improperly titled beneficiary form for the IRA could mean the difference of thousands of dollars of taxes. This is just one more reason to work with a financial professional, one who can strategically partner with an estate planning attorney to diligently check your decisions.

Estate planning is one of the areas that must be well planned out for a successful retirement. You might ask questions like, "Where do you want your money to go? How will it transition? What are the tax implications? What kind of care do you want?" All of these questions, and so many more, need to be thought through. It typically does not bode well for anyone if you allow your family to haggle over these details. Sometimes we hear, "Well, they can sort it out. . . . I won't be here anyway, so it doesn't matter to me where it all goes!"

Here are the facts. If your kids argued when they were little, they don't just magically stop, especially when money and property are concerned. This is never more true than when blended families come into play. When you start adding in step-parents, step-children, etc., things can get messy quickly.

Take the guesswork out. Do the responsible thing. Have an estate plan. Have your POA, medical directives, and will. Make sure you have updated beneficiaries. If you need a trust, have one, but only if you understand it and use it. In our professional experience, most people with trusts don't really understand why they have it.

The success of your overall estate plan is determined by how well your financial professional and attorney work together. We take so much pride in helping our clients understand this process. When you know you have all your ducks in a row, that's when you can enjoy retirement and be carefree!

CHAPTER 8

Money Perspective

When I was four years old, my grandparents gave me my very first piggy bank. It was made of metal, had a spring for a tail, and had a screw in the underside of the belly. I remember dropping coins in it and hearing the metal clang as the pieces rattled around. I quickly realized how easy it was to save, and how hard it was to actually get the money out to spend. The only way to ever retrieve the money was to unscrew the tiny little screw and then the piggy bank would come apart into two separate pieces.

Unfortunately, at that time I didn't know how to use a screwdriver. The best I could do was to violently shake the piggy bank upside down and hope something would pop out and land on the carpet. As I got older, I would do chores around the house. My parents taught me that my chores were my way to contribute to the family. However, from time to time I was given money for those chores. Again, I was told to save that money and take care of it, and then, when I wanted to buy something, I would have that money to use.

In high school and college, we were taught basic finances. One of the main lessons I continually heard was to create a budget. "Don't spend more than you make," one of my instructors said. All throughout our lives, we were taught how to save money. My grandparents, being from the Depression Era, told me to put money aside for a rainy day. Certain sayings like, "money doesn't grow on trees" and "a penny saved is a penny earned" were engrained in my psyche. I bet that's how it was for you, too.

However, what no one talks or teaches about is how to make your money last, and how to use it later on in life . . . in retirement, when you really need it. Our culture, our parents, our schools, and our society breeds us to look at our accounts and our money in only one way. We are taught to look at our accounts as we are saving and say to ourselves, "That is my 401(k). That is my life insurance. That is my IRA. That is my Roth IRA."

While all of those statements are true and accurate, those only describe what the accounts *are*. What we should really be asking ourselves is not what the accounts are BUT RATHER **what are those accounts going to be used for?** What will we be using the money on, later in life? The answer to that question typically is to *supplement* our income in retirement. To cover our healthcare and long-term care expenses. To pass on money to future generations. To give to charity. When you start asking yourself what your accounts and money will be used for rather than just identifying what they are, you will manage them completely differently.

Some accounts give you a one-time tax advantage when you put money in the account. Yes, those can be wonderful accounts to save in. Other accounts give you tax advantages, when you take the money out of the account . . . *forever*! Most times we save in a manner to get a temporary tax advantage on the front end while sacrificing a forever tax advantage on the back end. We take a temporary short-term advantage in place of a forever long-term advantage. When we think about what we want to use our money for, we can then better determine which types of accounts and advantages will best serve that purpose.

Shifting from being a saver with a steady paycheck and adding money into your accounts into being a spender, where the steady paychecks stop and money starts to flow out of your accounts, is quite a daunting and sometimes scary transition for most people. Since we know retirement is the stage of life we are building up to and saving for, wouldn't it make sense for us to start managing our finances and our accounts for that stage of life? The money you have saved to support you in the present moment are your bank accounts, your money market accounts, and your CDs. But the IRA, the Roth IRA, the 401(k), your life insurance, etc., these are there to support you when you don't have any other income. They need to be treated as such, and they need to be managed in that manner!

Women-Specific Concerns

I help men, women, and families from all walks of life on their journey to and through retirement. Yet, I want to address the female demographic specifically. Why? To be perfectly blunt, women are 35 percent more likely to deal with poverty than men.[42]

The topics, products, and strategies I cover elsewhere in this book are meant to help address retirement concerns for men and women, but those kinds of statistics are a reminder that much of traditional planning is geared toward men. Male careers, male lifespans, male healthcare. Women's career paths often look much different than men's, so why would their retirement strategies look the same?

I grew up in a *Leave It to Beaver* family. My mom, Deb, was a stay-at-home mom. My dad, Dwight, was a healthcare executive. He'd go off to work every day

---

[42] Amanda Fins. National Women's Law Center. December 2020. "National Snapshot: Poverty among Women & Families, 2020." https://nwlc.org/wp-content/uploads/2020/12/PovertySnapshot2020.pdf

from 6 a.m. to 6 p.m. I knew from an early age that wasn't going to be me. I was going to own my own business.

At age ten, I had a baseball card stand. At thirteen I sold fake tattoos at school. At twenty-two I was teaching little kids soccer lessons, and at twenty-eight, I got a dream job with AXA advisors, where my pay would finally be based on my sweat equity.

One night, soon after being hired, I needed a break from studying for all those financial tests, so I went to Mom's house.

As I watched her cooking the best pasta and meatballs ever, she said, "Scott, I know you're going to do great. And if there's ever anything I can do to help, just let me know."

Six weeks later, I was getting ready to go on my first appointment with my very first client. I drove to their house, pulled into the driveway, grabbed my leather briefcase, walked up to the door, and rang the doorbell.

"Hi Mom!" I said.

She led me into the formal dining room, the one we only use for Thanksgiving and Christmas dinners. *Man*, I remember thinking, *this feels weird*. In my family, we never talked about money with each other. I had absolutely no idea how much my mom got when she and my dad divorced.

I sat down at the dining room table and pulled out my questionnaire.

"Mom, how much do you have in savings?" She gave me a number. "That's all?" I asked. "Hmmm. Seems low. How much do you have in your retirement accounts?" Again, she gave me a pretty small number. Wow. I thought she would've had a lot more.

"Mom, when do you want to retire?"

As I looked up, I could see the tears starting to well up in her eyes. My first thought was that those financial tests I had taken six weeks prior never told me what to do when you are sitting across from your mom and she is crying about her money!

I asked her what was wrong.

"Well, when your father and I got divorced, I received some money. I didn't know what to do so I asked Julie. You know, Julie and Joe. We've been friends with them forever. Well, Julie told me they used Frank as their advisor, so I went to Frank, and he was very nice and seemed knowledgeable. So, I put my money with Frank, and the next thing I know I'm in court because Frank was stealing from me. I couldn't tell you about it."

"Hold on a minute..." I said, trying to process. "How much did you have?"

"$1 million."

"And how much did you lose?"

"$300,000!"

My immediate reaction was to find this Frank guy and rip his head off. Instead I said, "Mom, I'm going to handle this."

I immediately got back in the car and called Jeff, the best senior advisor at AXA. I drove back to the office at 6 p.m. on a Friday evening, and Jeff and I stayed up until 11 p.m. running the numbers and putting together a plan.

A week later I pulled up to Mom's again, grabbed my briefcase, rang the doorbell, and sat down at the dining room table.

"Mom, I have good news," I told her. "You can keep your standard of living, and you will not run out of money. The bad news? For that to happen, you're going to have to work ten more years until you're sixty-six.

"Okay," was all she said. I could see the disappointment written all over her face. But we both knew it was the best plan.

Every year, I'd meet with Mom and update her on where we were at with her plan, and I am so proud to finally say she has officially retired!

I share this story with you because, while my parents were married, my dad made most of the big financial decisions. Because of my mom's situation and many others, I have firsthand experience in helping and planning for the day one of the spouses becomes single. Whether it's from a divorce or death, it is frightening and requires careful design.

Be Informed

It's a familiar scene in many financial offices across the country: A woman comes into an appointment carrying a sack full of unopened envelopes. Often through tears, she sits across the desk from a financial professional and apologizes her way through a conversation about what financial products she owns and where her income is coming from. She is recently widowed and was sure her spouse was taking care of the finances, but now she doesn't know where all of their assets are kept, and her confidence in her financial outlook has wavered after walking through funeral expenses and realizing she's down to one income.

Often, she may be financially okay. Yet the uncertainty can be wearying, particularly when the family is already reeling from a loss. While this scenario sometimes plays out with men, in my experience, it's more likely to be a woman in that chair across the desk, probably in part because of Western traditions about money management being "a guy thing." But it doesn't have to be this way. This all-too-common scenario can be wiped away with just a little preparation.

Talk to Your Spouse/Work With a Financial Professional

While there are many factors affecting women's financial preparation for and situation in retirement, I cannot emphasize enough that the decision to be informed, to be a part of the conversation, and to be aware of what is going on with your finances is absolutely paramount to a confident retirement. With all of the couples I've seen, there is almost always an "alpha" when it comes to finances. It isn't always men— for many of my coupled clients, the wife is the alpha who keeps the books, budgets, and knows to the penny where all of the family's assets are—yet, statistically among baby boomers, it is usually a man who runs the books. But as time goes on, it looks like the ratio of male to female financial alphas is evening out. According to a Gallup study, women are equally as likely to take the lead on finances as men, with 37 percent of U.S. households showing women primarily paying the bills. Half of households also say decisions about savings and investments are shared equally.[43] Whether that's the way your household works or not,

[43] Megan Brenan. Gallup. January 29, 2020. "Women Still Handle Main Household Tasks in U.S." https://news.gallup.com/poll/283979/women-handle-main-household-tasks.aspx

there isn't anything wrong with that. The breakdown is when there is a lack of communication, when no one other than the financial alpha knows how much they have and where. In the end, it doesn't matter which person handles the money; it's all about all parties being informed of what's going on financially.

There are a lot of ways to open up the conversation about money. One woman I heard of started a conversation with her husband, the financial alpha, by sitting down and saying, "Teach me how to be a widow." Perhaps that sounds grim, but it was to the point, and it opened up what she said was a very fruitful conversation. The conversation opener that I often hear is when clients come to our office. Whether it's the financial alpha or the financial beta who set the first appointment, couples sometimes have their first real conversation about money, assets, and their retirement plans in our office. The important thing about having these conversations isn't where, it's when . . . and the best when is as soon as possible.

Spouse-Specific Options

One area where it might be especially important to be on the same page between spouses is when it comes to financial products or services that have spousal options. A few that come to mind are pensions and Social Security, although life insurance and annuity policies also have the potential to affect both spouses.

With pensions, taking the worker's life-only option is somewhat attractive—after all, the monthly payment is bigger. However, you and your spouse should discuss your options. When we're talking about both of you as opposed to just one lifespan, there is an increased likelihood that at least one of you will live a long, long time. That means the monthly payout will be less, but it also ensures that, no matter which spouse outlives the other, no one will have to suffer the loss of a needed pension paycheck in his or her later retirement years.

While we covered Social Security options in a different chapter, I think some of the spousal information bears repeating. Particularly, if you worked exclusively inside the home for a significant number of years, you may want to talk about taking your Social Security benefits based on your spouse's work history. After all, Social Security is based on your thirty-five highest-earning years.

Things to remember about the spousal benefits:[44]

- Your benefit will be calculated as a percentage (up to 50 percent) of your spouse's earned monthly benefit at his or her full retirement age, or FRA.
- For you to begin receiving a spousal benefit, your spouse must have already filed for his or her own benefits and you must be at least sixty-two.
- You can qualify for a full half of your spouse's benefits if you wait until you reach FRA to file.
- Beginning your benefits earlier than your FRA will reduce your monthly check but waiting to file until after FRA will not increase your benefits.

---

[44] Social Security Administration. "Retirement Planner: Benefits For You As A Spouse."
https://www.ssa.gov/planners/retire/applying6.html

For divorcees:[45]

- You may qualify for an ex-spousal benefit if . . .
  a. You were married for a decade or more
  b. *and* you are at least sixty-two
  c. *and* you have been divorced for at least two years
  d. *and* you are currently unmarried
  e. *and* your ex-spouse is sixty-two (qualifies to begin taking Social Security)
- Your ex-spouse does not need to have filed for you to file on his or her benefit.
- Similar to spousal benefits, you can qualify for up to half of your ex-spouse's benefits if you wait to file until your FRA.
- If your ex-spouse dies, you may file to receive a widow/widower benefit on his or her Social Security record as long as you are at least age sixty and fulfill all the other requirements on the preceding alphabetized list.
  a. This will not affect the benefits of your ex-spouse's current spouse

For widow's (or widower's, for that matter) benefits:[46]

- You may qualify to receive as much as your deceased spouse would have received if . . .
  a. You were married for at least nine months before his or her death

---

[45] Social Security Administration. "Retirement Planner: If You Are Divorced."
https://www.ssa.gov/planners/retire/divspouse.html
[46] Social Security Administration. "Survivors Planner: If You Are The Worker's Widow Or Widower."
https://www.ssa.gov/planners/survivors/ifyou.html#h2

      b. *or* you would qualify for a divorced spousal benefit

      c. *and* you are at least sixty

      d. *and* you did not/have not remarried before age sixty

- You may earn delayed credits on your spouse's benefit *if* your spouse hadn't already filed for benefits when he or she died.
- Other rules may apply to you if you are disabled or are caring for a deceased spouse's dependent or disabled child.

Longevity

On average, women live longer than men. Most stats put average female longevity at about two years more than men. But averages are tricky things. An April 2022 report by the World Economic Forum listed the eight oldest people in the world to all be women. They ranged in age from 118 years old to 114 and included two Americans.[47]

On one hand, this is a Rosie the Riveter moment. How fabulous are ladies? On the other hand, this reveals longstanding financial ramifications.

For me to find an example of this, I have to look no further than my grandmother, Shirley. She was born in 1927 and her husband, my grandfather, passed away in 1989. As of the writing of this book, she just celebrated her ninety-second birthday, outliving her husband by

---

[47] Martin Armstrong. World Economic Forum. April 29, 2022. "How old are the world's oldest people?" https://www.weforum.org/agenda/2022/04/the-oldest-people-in-the-world

more than thirty years. Women live longer than men, and we must plan for the uncertainties that brings.

Simply Needing More Money in Retirement

Living longer in retirement means needing more money, period. Barring a huge lottery win or some crazy stock market action, the date you retire is likely the point at which you have the most money you will ever have. Not to put too grim a spin on it, but the problem with longevity is, the further you get away from that date, the further your dollars have to stretch. If you planned to live to a nice eighty-something, but you live to a nice one-hundred-something, that is TWO DECADES you will need to account for, monetarily.

To put this in perspective, let's say you like to drink coffee as an everyday splurge. Not accounting for inflation or leap years, a $2.50 cup-a-day habit is $18,250 over a two-decade span. Now think of all the things you like to do that cost money. Add those up for twenty years of unanticipated costs. I think you'll see what I mean.

More Health Care Needs

In addition to the cost of living for a longer lifespan is the fact aging, plain and simple, means more health care, and more health care means more money. Women are survivors. They suffer from the morbidity-mortality paradox, which states women suffer more non-fatal illnesses throughout their lifetime than men, who experience fewer illnesses but higher mortality.

Women have been found to seek treatment more often when not feeling well and emphasize staying healthy when older, according to studies.[48] So survival is on the side of the woman. However, surviving things, like cancer, also means more checkups later in life.

Widowhood

Not only do women typically live longer than their same-age male counterparts, they also have the tendency to marry men older than themselves. The numbers bear this out: Worldwide, one in five women live in a solo household after turning sixty compared to one in ten men.[49]

I don't write this to scare people; rather, I think it's fundamentally important to prepare my female clients for something that may be a startling, *but very likely,* scenario. At some point, most women will have to handle their financial situations on their own. A little preparation can go a long way, and having a basic understanding of your household finances and the "who, what, where, and how much" of your family's assets is incredibly useful—it can prevent a tragic situation from being more traumatic.

In my opinion, the financial services industry sometimes underserves women in these situations.

48 advisory.com. July 22, 2020. "Why do women live longer than men? It's more complicated than you think." https://www.advisory.com/en/daily-briefing/2020/07/22/longevity

49 Jacob Ausubel. Pew Research Center. January 3, 2020. "Globally, women are younger than their male partners, more likely to age alone" https://www.pewresearch.org/fact-tank/2020/01/03/globally-women-are-younger-than-their-male-partners-more-likely-to-age-alone

Some financial professionals tend to alienate women, even when their spouses are alive. I've heard several stories of women who sat through meeting after meeting without their financial professional ever addressing a single question to them.

In our firm, when we work with couples, we work hard to make sure our retirement income strategies work for *both* people. No matter who the financial alpha is, it's important for everyone affected by a retirement strategy to understand it.

We met Ted and Barbara about a year ago. When we met them, they were working with another advisor. They came to us the way most folks do, wanting some help and a second opinion to make sure they weren't overlooking anything. As we guided them through our retirement planning process and put together their plan, Barbara made the comment that she felt like we really were paying attention to her. She mentioned how nice it was to feel honored and heard. She told us their other advisor just assumed Ted made all the decisions and really only ever looked at him in their meetings.

We could tell she really wasn't comfortable with their current advisor. That broker was mostly disregarding Barbara as a having a non-role in the planning and the finances. It is imperative you partner with someone who understands the nuances of planning for couples, widows/widowers, and single people alike. In our firm, we go to great lengths to make sure both spouses feel honored and served in the retirement planning process.

When we work with couples, we work hard to make sure our retirement income strategies work for both people. No matter who is the financial alpha, it's important for everyone who is affected by a retirement plan to understand it.

When we met Christina, she had been widowed for a few years. Her husband, Troy, had passed away from cancer, and Christina cared for him in his illness. For most of their marriage, they were middle-class and worked to provide for their two children. They had what most considered the "all-American" family.

As part of their financial planning, Troy had done the right thing and made sure that if anything ever happened to him, Christina would be taken care of. He had several million dollars of life insurance to cover his salary and the Social Security check Christina wouldn't receive after his death. With the cancer diagnosis being terminal, Christina unfortunately knew these policies would be used by her and not her children. When Troy finally passed away, she inherited the life insurance money. As you might imagine, going from a middle-class income to several millions of dollars comes with major stress and responsibility. Also, having to make these important financial decisions on her own without Troy to be there as her sounding board to make the decisions was a source of great concern.

When we had our first visit, she shared with us that Troy had made most of the decisions around their finances. She really didn't know what to do and who to turn to. It was completely overwhelming for her to assume this role, and she was very concerned about spending too much money. She didn't' want to run out of it.

Having worked with many widows and widowers over the course of our careers, our team was able to put together a plan that addressed her needs and goals while making sure the strategies were tailored to life as a single person and no longer as part of a married couple. One of the main things about this type of planning is making sure you're able to have the type of care you want if you have to take care of yourself without a spouse to depend on. The next thing we'll talk about is making sure you have a solid tax plan.

Taxes

One of the pieces of widowhood that often comes unexpectedly is the tax bill. Many women continue similar lifestyles to the ones they shared with their spouses. This, in turn, means continuing to have a similar need for income. However, after the death of a spouse, their taxes will be calculated based on a single filer's income table, which is much less forgiving than the couple's tax rates. With proper planning, your financial professional and tax advisor may be able to help you take the sting out of your new tax status.

Caregiving

Of the 53 million caregivers providing unpaid, informal care for older adults in 2020, 61 percent are women. Among today's family caregivers, 61 percent work and 45 percent report some kind of financial impact from providing a loved one care and support.[50] In addition to the financial burden created by caregiving responsibilities, women devote an average of 5.7 hours each day to duties such as housekeeping and looking

---

[50] caregiving.org. 2020 Report. "Caregiving in the U.S. 2020." https://www.caregiving.org/caregiving-in-the-us-2020

after loved ones. [51] So then, when can women find the time to focus long and hard on financial matters?

I don't repeat these statistics to scare you. Estimates typically place the monetary value of unofficial caregiving services across the United States at around $150 billion or more. Yet, I think the emotional value of care that many women provide their elderly relatives or neighbors cannot be quantified with a number. So, to be clear, this shouldn't be taken as a "why not to provide caregiving." Instead, it should be seen as a call for "why to *prepare* for caregiving" or "how to lessen the financial and emotional burden of caregiving."

Funding Your Own Retirement

Specifically because of the aforementioned reasons, women need to be prepared to fund more of their own retirements. There are several savings options and products, including the spousal 401(k). Unlike a traditional 401(k), where you contribute money to a plan with your employer, a spousal 401(k) is something your spouse sets up on your behalf, so he can contribute a portion of his paycheck to your retirement funds. This is something to consider, particularly for families where one spouse has dropped out of the workforce to care for a relative.

Also, if you find yourself in a caregiving role, talk to your employer's human resources professional. Some companies have paid leave, special circumstance, or sick leave options you could qualify for, making it

---

[51] Drew Weisholtz. Today. January 22, 2020. "Women do 2 more hours of housework daily than men, study says." https://www.today.com/news/women-do-2-more-hours-housework-daily-men-study-says-t172272

easier to cope and possibly helping you stay in the workforce longer.

Saving Money

Women need more money to fund their retirements, period. But this doesn't have to be a significant burden—most of the time, women are better at saving, while usually taking less risk in their portfolios.[52] This gives me reason to believe, as women get more involved in their finances, families will continue to be better-prepared for retirement, both *his* and *hers*.

---

[52] Maurie Backman. The Motley Fool. March 4, 2021. "A Summary of 20 Years of Research and Statistics on Women in Investing." https://www.fool.com/research/women-in-investing-research

About the Author

Scott Winstead began his financial services career with AXA Advisors in 2009, after previously holding several leadership positions at a global healthcare firm. While working with a wide variety of clients during his first year as an advisor, Scott realized he very much enjoyed helping people create and manage their retirement plans.

It did not take long for Scott to realize proper planning and education are what make the difference between people having the retirement they envision or running out of money. Unfortunately, this type of planning is very specialized, and many consider it to be an overwhelming, time-consuming hassle. With that in mind, Scott founded Compass Retirement and designed his practice to help pre-retirees and retirees formulate solid plans to secure their financial futures.

Along with being distinguished as a Certified Education Consultant (CEC®) designee, Scott has passed the Series 7, 63, and 65 securities exams and holds a life, health and annuity license in Texas (license No. 1608033). He has the pleasure of speaking all over the Dallas/Fort Worth area through the Foundation for Financial Education (F3E), a nonprofit organization dedicated to providing free educational resources to the public.

Scott lives in Colleyville, Texas, with his wife, Angela, and enjoys hunting and fishing in his spare time. As a former Division I collegiate soccer athlete, he loves all things related to physical fitness and sports, including coaching his two children's teams. He has a deep appreciation for improving his cooking skills and spending quality time with his wife, family, and friends over a great meal.

www.ingramcontent.com/pod-product-compliance
Lightning Source LLC
Chambersburg PA
CBHW070233180526
45158CB00001BA/462